Continually inhabited for over 9,000 years, the island of Newfoundland rises from the white-capped waves of the North Atlantic as testament to the collective hard work, determination, and ingenuity of its peoples.

Roland L. Noël has spent much of his life contemplating the livelihoods and fortunes of these ancestors, first, growing up in Freshwater, Conception Bay, and later as custodian of his family tree. He blends firsthand knowledge, with the color and texture of daydreams, to paint a tapestry of the people of this island. Some call Newfoundland, "The Rock": Roland knows it as *A Place Called Home*.

Day Dreams
and
A Place Called Home

Freshwater, Conception Bay North
Newfoundland and Labrador, Canada

Roland L. Noël

Copyright © 2017 Roland L. Noël

All rights reserved. No part of this book may be reproduced or transmitted by any means, graphic, electronic or mechanical, including photocopying, recording, scanning or by any other information storage and retrieval system, without permission in writing from the author.

ISBN: 978-0-692-97415-5

All pictures in this book are the sole property of the owners and are protected by this book's copyright.

The copyright for the three poems not written by me are the sole property of the individual authors and may not be copied or used without their permission.

The copyright for the art work belongs to Brad Forward; it cannot be copied or used without permission.

e-mail Address: a-place-called-home@juno.com

Blurb-provided layout designs and graphic elements are copyright Blurb Inc., 2017. This book was created using the Blurb Creative Publishing Service and the book's author retains sole copyright to his or her contributions.

Poems in this book written by other authors:

THE FACE OF THE DEVIL		*Suzanne Fitzpatrick*		*page 15*

A DAY TO REMEMBER		*Hannah Dwyer*		*page 50*

OH, I JUST SAW A SIGHT		*Samuel Bernstein*		*page 55*

THE PROVINCIAL GRAND LODGE SESSION
				Unknown Author		*page 165*

ARTWORK				*Brad Forward*		*pages 9, 21*

All photographs are by the author except where noted.

Introduction

This book contains poems I have written over the years. I began writing as a young boy attending school in Freshwater, Conception Bay North, Newfoundland and Labrador, Canada.

I spent a lot of my time in the classroom daydreaming. I enjoyed both History and English Literature, but I especially enjoyed reading poetry.

To me history was adventurous: men sailed the seven seas to claim new lands, climbed the highest mountains and flew the endless skies on wings. In my daydreams I envisioned I was there where wars were fought and battles won and lost.

For most of my teenage years, Mr. Clayton Peach was my teacher and he made poetry come alive. I felt that I was a character in the adventure. It was in this atmosphere that I learned to enjoy poetry.

Soon my daydreams took control and I started writing poems about the people, places and stories I had heard. Often in my dreams, I sailed great ships, engaged in major battles around the world, climbed its highest mountain peaks and flew my aircraft on lofted wings over the war-torn skies of London, as I had read about in the history books.

In my daydreams I walked life's lonely highways, met people in despair, and saw the mighty oceans crash on life's rocky shore, heard the call of nature on a blistering winter's day and saw the lonely woodsman, trotting home in the shadows of a fading evening sun. I became a character of my own imagination and this book is the product of my daydreams.

I invite you to come along for the ride and share in the glorification of the daydreams of my past.

Acknowledgements

I would like to thank all those who helped make this book possible; my family and friends who gave me encouragement.

A special thanks to my wife, Eve (Christopher) Noel, who encouraged me to place these poems in a book and for her endless patience keeping me focused when editing and proofreading. Thanks to my brother-in-law, Dennis Flanders, for editing and proofreading and for restoring and improving some of my pictures that were old and faded; Leslie (Noel) Forward for sharing her invaluable knowledge of the Newfoundland Regiments in World Wars I and II; and Suzanne Fitzpatrick for editing and proofreading.

Thanks to the following who gave me permission to use their personal photos:

Gee (Noel) Dwyer, Charles Davis Noel, Dennis Flanders, Eve (Christopher) Noel, Peter Noel, Hannah Dwyer, Sylvia (Parsons) Pelley, Bonnie (Russell) Gillette, Joseph G. Noel, Audrey Maciel, Bonnie (Noel) Mousney, Valerie Noel, Charlie Butt, Jim Arpan, Derm Chafe, Glenys (Noel) Flanders, Beverley Noel, Herbert Davis, Frank Gogos, David Parsons and Brad Forward for his art work.

I would like to thank the following people from Archives, Museums and news outlets for their help in obtaining pictures and copyright licence:

Newfoundland

Don Tate - Newfoundland Grand Banks Genealogy Site
Allison Miller - Grand Falls-Windsor Heritage Society
Frank Gogos - *The Veteran Magazine*

N.B. Frank Gogos is the author of two books pertaining to the Royal Newfoundland Regiment:

<u>The Royal Newfoundland Regiment in the Great War</u>
A Guide to the Battlefields and Memorials of France, Belgium, and Gallipoli.
<u>Known Unto God</u>
The Newfoundland armed forces suffered devastating losses during World War I. Known unto God is a memorial to the men in these forces who died during the war and who have no known graves.

Canada

Susan Ross - Canadian War Museum

Kate Murphy - Media Relations, Veterans Affairs

Martin Ruddy - Reference Services Division/Library and Archives

Chris Lund - National Film Board of Canada/Library and Archives

United States of America

Ken LaRock - National Museum of the U.S. Air Force

Cate T. Mueller - U.S. Naval History & Heritage Command

Holly Reed - National Archives & Records Administration Still Picture

United Kingdom

Steven Rogers - Commonwealth War Graves Commission

Peter Elliott - Head of Archives, Royal Air Force Museum

Sophy Moynagh - Sales & Services Executive, Imperial War Museum

George Lanham - Production Manager DIVER Group Magazine – Eaton Publication, UK, for giving me permission to use and reprint the article about the HMS Othello II from Kendall McDonald's Book (*Dive Kent: A Diver Guide*).

In memory of my parents, sister and grandparents

Edward A. P. (Ted) Noel & Mabel P. (Butt) Noel

Beverley Marie Noel

George A. & Gertrude (Parsons) Noel

Charles & Laura (Burke) Butt

Index To Poems

	PAGE
Let Stand the Word Memorial	1
Heroes of My Hometown	11
The Face of the Devil	15
To the Boys of My Hometown	16
As the Sun Was Beacon Red	19
My Daddy Was a Pilot	24
Her Airman is Down	27
Forever Canada	31
They Were Seven	32
Forget-Us-Not	40
Christmas Peace	41
A Day to Remember	50
Oh, I Just Saw a Sight	55
The Long Flight Home	59
A Marine From the Fields of Vietnam	63
The Young Soldiers	69
A Month Of Remembrance	70
The Old Veteran	72
September 11, 2001	74
Our Ancestors	78
Historical Freshwater	83
Places That Were	88
I Dreamed in A Dream	95
It's Nights Like This	99
The Long Wait	100
In the Shadow of the Tolt	109
She Saw Not Life	113
Freshwater Stood Unconquered	121
The Lovely Antoinette	130
An Old Man's Tale	133
Let Not the Winds Blow, Lord	135
Somewhere Tonight Lost	138
A Sad Christmas Day	142
Under the Stars of Night	144

Sunset and Billowing Waves	146
Sir Wilfred Grenfell	148
Life's Blind Night	149
Oh, Foolish Youth	149
This I Call My Island Home	150
In the Shadows of Even	151
The One Lost Tribe	152
They Were Men of Courage	154
God Is My Co-Pilot	157
When the Clock Stops Ticking	158
Away from Home	159
A Light in The Valley	160
The Robin Red Breast	161
Life's Story Book	162
Give Me A Home In Newfoundland	163
God Ne'er Let Us Forget	163
The Provincial Grand Lodge Session	165
Life's Mountain	168
What Is Life?	169
My Beacon Light	171
I Must Walk This Path Alone	172
Thank You Mom	174
Thank You Dad	175
In the Winds of An Autumn Breeze	177
Freshwater Community Reunion, August 4th, 2000	182

Day Dreams

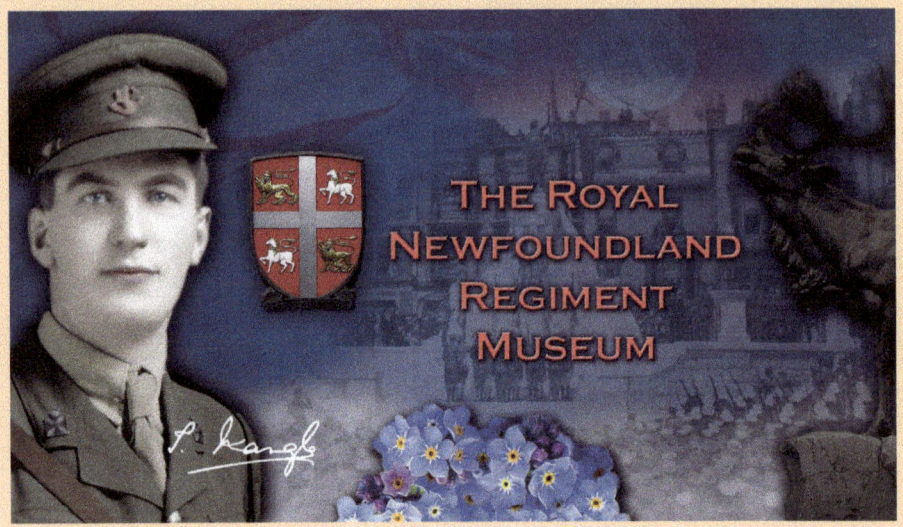
Photo by Frank Gogos

The Veteran Magazine

World War I

The Fighting Newfoundlander

Bowring Park, St. John's, NL

So We Might Live in Freedom

Bowring Park, St. John's, NL

*In memory of those who paid the supreme sacrifice
and all the men and women of Freshwater who served their country.*

Let Stand The Word Memorial

February 16, 1961

Come ye student Newfoundlanders
And listen to what I say,
It is about our soldier boys
For us, a sacrifice did pay.

Newfoundland to Queenston Heights
You will find their names well known,
While in the defense of Canada
Great courage they had shown.

'Twas in the days of young Canada
When home armies were unknown,
'Twas in the days of musket volley
They answered back each tone.

Newfoundland helped save Canada
From rebels across the border,
When the War of twelve* was o'er
Her name was set in mortar.

In nineteen hundred and fourteen
When Kaiser shook the world,
Each member of this regiment
Into blue and khaki hurled.

All soldiers of this regiment --
Was made up of volunteers --
When Europe clashed into war
She joined with hopes and fears.

From Newfoundland to Gallipoli
Great waters they did span,

---

* *War of 1812*

Leaving pen and books back home
They were sons of Newfoundland.

When crossing the Dardanelles
They left a gory trail behind,
A trail marked by drops of red
Today if you look, you'll find.

Their markers lying side by side
With poppies blowing between,
Look with careful thought
Of infernal days they'd seen.

England to Beaumont Hamel
Their blood did freely flow,
At the Battle of the Somme
Great courage they did show.

It was an early July morning
As the sun rose in the east,
A regiment crouched in trenches
Like hunters pursuing a beast.

It was in a dawning twilight
When buglers sounded charge,
Our men went over the top
Through an artillery barrage.

But as evening shadowed
With a dimming sunset low,
Out there in no man's land
Priceless blood did flow.

Eight Hundred and one
Went into the battle strong,
Next morn sixty-eight answered roll
O God, what had gone wrong?

The soldiers were caught in crossfire
Those boys of our island home,
Advancing with their comrades
They died on blood soaked loam.

Star shells were bursting brighter
As they crawled through gaps of wire,
They fought with incredible courage
As they raced through walls of fire.

The men were haggard and worn
Yet their pace resisted to tire,
Strongmen raced to the front line
While wounded crawled in mire.

They fought all day in a blazing sun
Soon the air reeked of death,
Charging across the killing fields
They defied the foe they met.

Blood ran free on the Caribou Trail
A trail no man dare retract,
It was blazed by life's young tide
Of men who would not turn back.

They wore the badge of the caribou
An ensign worn with pride,
In the midst of encounters
The word surrender: denied.

The greatest trail they ever trod --
I will tell you where and when --
It was not the trail of the water span
Nor the grassy meadows fen.

It was the trail of a silent heart
A heart that would not yield,
That left its physical form to die
On a blood soaked battlefield.

It was haunting thoughts of home
The friends they left behind,
Memories of boyhood days
As smoke, conflict entwined.

Thoughts of a mother's love --
A love which is divine,
That no man can explain --
Was the love left behind.

It was thoughts of comrades dead
And men who had gone before,
Fighting with fearful hearts
The greatest battle they ever saw.

They suffered along the trail
This trail of death and pain,
Not all from physical fight,
But also from mental strain.

Theirs is a trail no men will tread
For it was trod by our fallen dead,
We must keep this trail cut clear,
All they had, with us did share.

They lived, died, gave their all --
Do not ever let their memory fall,
For when the sun rose in the east
It was not good for man, nor beast.

When evening sun sank in the west
They proved better than the best,
For when the combat drew to an end,
The Caribou Trail was a slaughter pen.

Come think, think, think if you will
Of men and boys who knew no bound,
Lived, fought and died in a rising sun,
Now they lie in some foreign ground.

Let Memorial University be hallowed land
Their names engraved immemorial,
It was for this Island, they took their stand
Let stand the word: Memorial.

PA-128014.   National Film Board of Canada/Library and Archives

Memorial University of Newfoundland was built in 1928 and dedicated to the Royal Newfoundland Regiment and its fallen heroes. In 1961, I read a newspaper article of a movement to omit "Memorial" and rename it University of Newfoundland. This inspired me to write this poem.

The Battle of the Somme 1916
After the advance of the Newfoundland Regiment at Beaumont Hamel on July 1st, Major Arthur Raley reported:

"The only visible sign that the men knew they were under this terrific fire was that they instinctively tucked their chins into an advanced shoulder as they had done so often when fighting their way home against a blizzard of snow in some little outport in far off Newfoundland..."

Imperial War Museum, UK

Sir John R. B. Bennett, Newfoundland Minister of the Militia, inspecting troops of the Royal Newfoundland Regiment at Ecuires, France, 25 June 1918.

Entrance to Beaumont Hamel Newfoundland Memorial, John Oxenham poem:

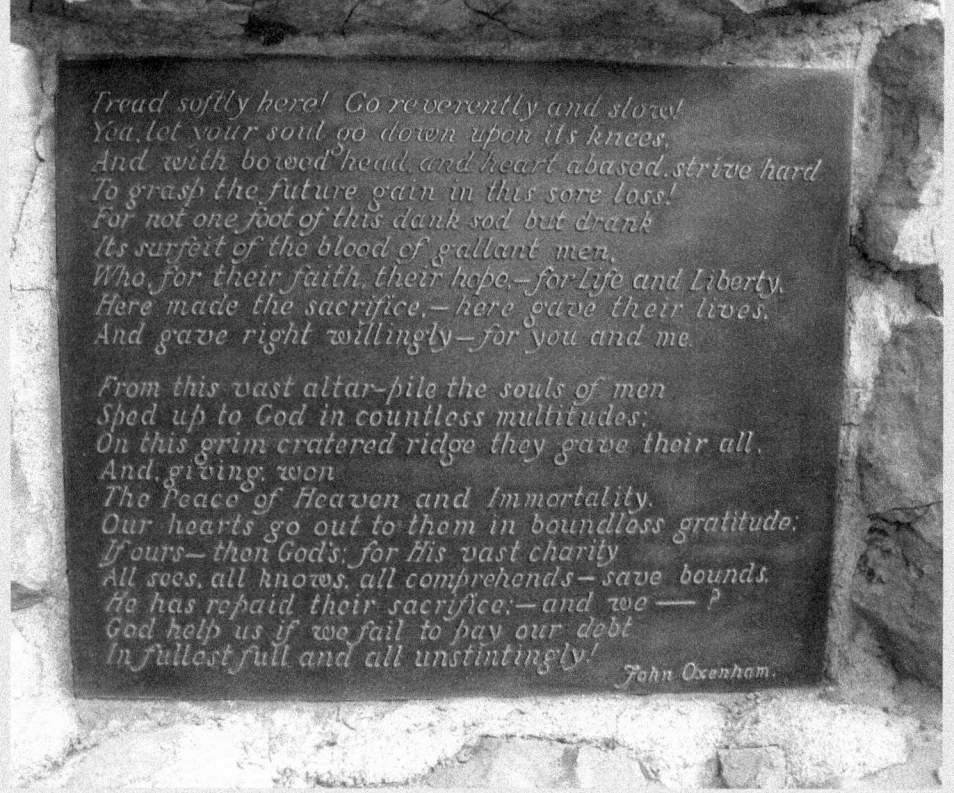

Photo by Peter Noel

The Killing Fields

Photos by Peter Noel

© *Commonwealth War Graves Commission, UK*

L/C Samuel J. Moores, who took part in the battle of the Somme, was killed in action October 12, 1916 at the Battle of Guedecourt, France. His body was never recovered. His name is displayed on the Beaumont Hamel Monument Memorial which contains the names of soldiers who have no known graves.

In From The Killing Fields

The Blue Puttees Beaumont Hamel
Battle of the Somme July 1, 1916
© Blue Is The Colour
Artist Brad Forward

Permission of the artist Brad Forward

During World War I, the Newfoundland Regiment, 801 strong, was under the command of the British Army. On the morning of July 1, 1916 as the Battle of the Somme began, the Newfoundland Regiment received orders to take the town of Beaumont Hamel. Eighty men were left in reserve, and 721 Newfoundlanders went over the top; of those, the most cited number is 310 dead and missing on the battlefield. We do not know the exact number of men who died that morning - we may never know - for some took four days to come in off the field and some died in hospital days later. We do know the morning after the battle only sixty-eight answered roll call. The regiment suffered a ninety-one percent casualty rate.

In recognition of the unit's valour after the Battle of Ypres, King George V bestowed the regiment with the prefix "Royal" on September 28, 1917, renaming them as the Royal Newfoundland Regiment. This was the only time during the First World War that this honour was given and only the third time in the history of the British Army that it has been given during a time of war: the last occasion was 101 years earlier.

Commander Brigadier-General Cayley of the 88th Brigade wrote Prime Minister of Newfoundland, Sir Edward Morris, quoting Major-General Sir Beauvoir de Lisle, Commander of the 29th British Division, reporting on the efforts of the 1st Newfoundland Regiment:

"It was a magnificent display of trained and disciplined valour, and its assault only failed of success because dead men can advance no further."

Canadian Soldiers Going Over The Top
1916

PA-000648©

Photo courtesy of
Barbara Noel Drover
Ernest Moores

Library and Archives Canada

Ernest Moores from Freshwater served in the Royal Highlanders Canadian Scottish Regiment. He was wounded at the Battle of the Somme, but recovered to return to the front lines. He survived the war and lived to old age.

Heroes of My Hometown
1957

Come think, and think of it well,
Of boys who heard the old school bell,
In a school yard where they played and ran,
Singing in a country band.

For they were lads just out of school,
With no experience in trade or tool,
Yet, they were lads -- the lads so brave --
For king and country their lives gave.

They were lads who answered the call,
To see that tyrants of Axis fall,
Joining army, navy or air force,
Each man plotted his future course.

Some crossed o'er land, others, the sea,
To keep this world peaceful and free.
Now many young men are lying at rest,
They fought the good fight and did their best.

God in his mercy, He understood,
And formed for them a brotherhood,
To live forever with Him on high
It was for our freedoms they did die.

May God inscribe on his golden wall.
The names of those who answered the call.

© *Commonwealth War Graves Commission, UK*

DOVER (ST. JAMES'S) CEMETERY, UK

The resting place of Ordinary Seaman Frederick J. Butt who lost his life on the HM Othello II. (See picture next page.)

Newfoundland Royal Naval Reserve
The Othello II Crew
1915

Photo courtesy of Leslie Noel Forward

Sailors in Training on the HMS Victory before joining the Othello II. Back row: second from the left, Frederick J. Butt and second from right, George A. Noel -- two boys from Freshwater.

HMS Trawler Othello II

© WW I Armed HMS Trawler Othello II, A Minefield Victim

HMS Othello II. This 206 ton armed Admiralty trawler was No. 1193 and part of the Dover minesweeping force when she became yet another victim of UC - 6's October 30 minefield. On October 31, 1915, she was ordered by Commander W.G. Rigg, the Minesweeping Officer, Dover, to move to "Section Two" which was the code for the area between the Goodwin Gate and the Gull Light Ship. It was as she battled to get there against a strong gale from the south-south-east that she hit a mine at 11:55 a.m. The explosion broke her nearly in two and she started sinking immediately. The wheelhouse was so distorted by the explosion that neither the door nor the windows would open.

Trapped inside as the water rose up around them were the skipper, the second-in-command (the "second hand"), the helmsman and a deck boy. The three men managed to squeeze the boy out of a partly open window, but could not follow themselves. The boy was the only one saved out of the ten aboard. (See Site 220*.) As a result of this incident, orders were given to remove all the sliding doors of the trawlers' wheelhouses and to replace them with canvas screens which could be pushed out in an emergency. This is said to have saved a number of lives in later sinkings.

Today, the Othello II lies at 51 08 04 N; 01 24 40 E with her bow to the east in 27m, though a scour increases that to 29m, of water. The wreck is about 30m long and stands 5m proud. She has been positively identified by her builder's plate.

© Reproduced from Dive Kent with permission of Underwater World Publications Ltd, UK
* Dive Sites Area 3, location 220 see page 188

The Face Of The Devil
© The Song of George Noel
Suzanne Fitzpatrick

This is my story and I'll tell you it true,
we were two fisherman who wanted to do
our part in the Great War so we signed on
for a year with the navy and sailed from St. John's.

We were on the *Othello*, a rusty old tub,
it had plenty of leaks and lousy old grub;
it went into dry dock to have some work done,
I was glad to be off her, I'll tell you my son.

So my mate Fred Butt and I came to be
on the crew of the Excellence, Royal Navy.
Then the time came when we had to choose --
I knew in my heart the *Othello* would lose.

I said to Fred, Why not stay with me?
but the Othello was where he wanted to be;
we said our good-byes and we left him behind,
and sailed through rough waters heavily mined.

Just a few nights later while far out to sea,
I dreamt that old Fred was right there with me,
Would you like a cup of tea now, George? he said,
and when I looked up, I felt total dread.

George A. Noel

For there by my berth, standing so close to me
was my old friend Fred, with a hot cup of tea,
but the face of the Devil was on him that night
After *Othello* was mined and sank out of sight.

This poem retells my grandfather George Albert Noel's true story. The HMS Othello II hit a mine and sank on October 31, 1915. All hands were lost - including his friend Fred Butt - except a cabin boy who was small enough to escape through a smashed porthole.

Suzanne Fitzpatrick
from <u>Washed Away</u>
2007

To The Boys Of My Hometown
April 28, 1958

Here's to the boys of my hometown,
That now sleep under foreign ground.
They took their place upon the strand,
Fought and died for Newfoundland.

Sleep on, sleep on, soldier boys,
You answered to the bugle cries.

You were the boys of my hometown,
Who into manhood quickly grown.
When trumpets were sounding war,
You were the first to leave our shore.

Sleep on, sleep on, forestry boys,
Let your axes fall and rise.

You were boys on our squid ground,
Where squid juice was flying around.
You were our youth upon the blues,
The paddle oar with skill could use.

Sleep on, sleep on, sailor boys,
While the tides do fall and rise.

You were our boys of youth and prime,
And flew your planes with skill sublime.
You are remembered far and wide,
We now play where you would run and slide.

Sleep on, sleep on, flier boys,
You are the guardians of our skies.

We walk the streets where you have walked,
Talked the talk that you once talked.
We attend school where you all went,
There many a weary hour spent.

Sleep on, sleep on, in your adopted land,
For King and country, you made your stand.

The Fate Of The Emden

German Battle Ship

*See page 189

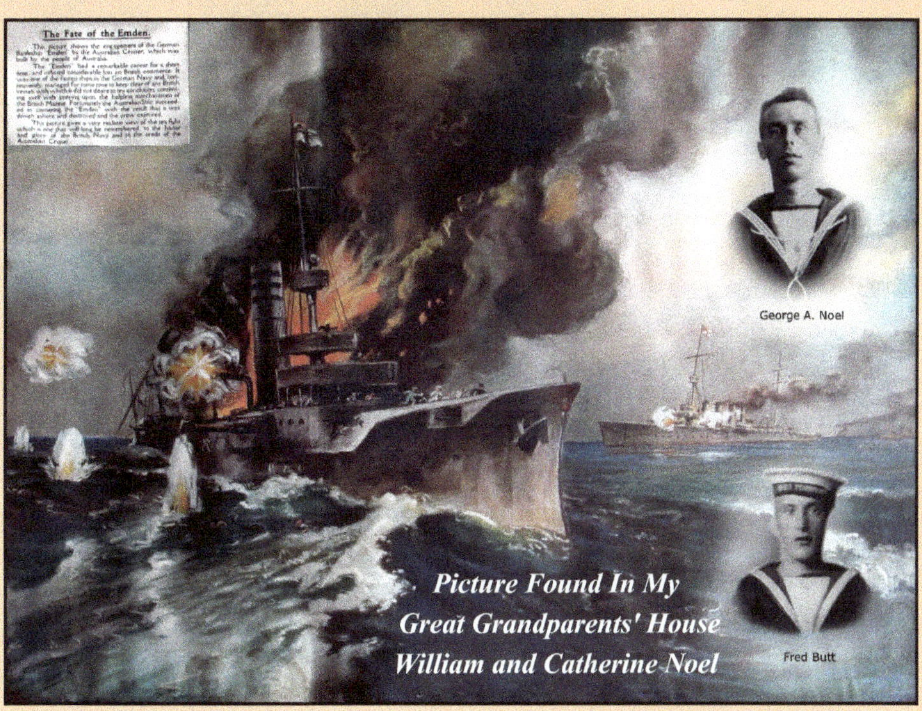
The Fate of the Emden.
George A. Noel
Picture Found In My
Great Grandparents' House
William and Catherine Noel
Fred Butt

Sailors inserted by Dennis Flanders

Two friends from Freshwater joined the Navy together and served on the Othello II. George A. Noel survived the war.

From These Waters They Became Sailors

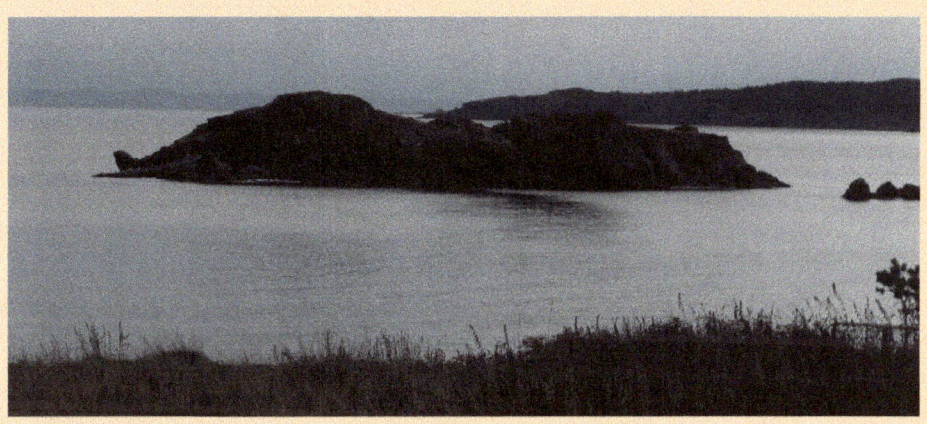

Beaumont Hamel - The Battle Of The Somme
July 1, 1916

© *Veterans Affairs Canada*
Canadian Virtual Memorial

Private SILAS JEFFERS

Photo by Peter Noel

Peter at Silas Jeffers's gravestone in the Newfoundland Cemetery at Beaumont Hamel, France.

In Memory
Privates Silas Jeffers, Ernest Moores, and L/Cpl. Samuel Moores

Private Jeffers died July 1, 1916 at The Danger Tree as he advanced across the fields of Beaumont Hamel during the Battle of the Somme in France.

"Silas died facing the enemy is proved by the fact that the note book and Bible which he carried in front of his breast pocket were shot through."
The Freshwater Recorder, Vol. 1 November 1918, No. 3

As a young boy growing up in Freshwater I had the privilege of seeing the book and Bible, along with a handkerchief, he had in his breast pocket. The bullet passed through all three items. In addition, it inspired me to write the poem "As the Sun Was Beacon Red".

Two other soldiers from Freshwater were on the field that day: L/Cpl. Samuel Moores and Pte. Ernest Moores. Samuel Moores was killed in action October 12, 1916 at the Battle of Guedecourt, France. Later that year Ernest Moores was wounded, but returned to the lines.

As The Sun Was Beacon Red
1958

On a battlefield in far off France
That first day of July,
While waiting for the zero hour,
We heard the charging cry.

Eight Hundred and one
Out of the trenches came,
Not one of us there knowing
Our battle was making fame.

Here I was in the trenches
With a young lad by my side,
I heard him when he whistled,
I heard him when he cried.

I heard this young soldier
As he said his prayers at night,
Praying to God to care for Mother,
Ought he to die in morning fight.

Heard him talk of his mother,
The best in the world he'd say,
"I will love her with all my heart,
Until the great Judgement Day."

We fought side by side in Gallipoli
Where many a comrade fell,
We prayed and cried in silence,
Running through a man-made hell.

He was a great companion
The best that one could ask,
But it was like a fleeting dream
With an ending approaching fast.

It was an early July morning
With the sun beacon red,
All around from left to right,
Death haggard overhead.

It was later in the killing field
I saw him go o'er the top.
And before my horrid eyes
Saw his fatal body drop.

Dashing forward we got him
But said, "It is too late,
I am going to meet my father,
He's waiting at the Pearly Gate."

He said, "Dear comrades,
It is not a losing fight,
For if you would keep pressing
You'll be in Hamel* by night."

Then in a lowly voice he said,
"May I ask this one request?
You will let my mother know
The place where now I rest."

Like a soldier brave and true
He slowly closed his eyes,
With these parting words he said,
"May God be with you, boys."

We laid him sad and slowly
Within a blood drenched grave,
This young lad of sixteen years,
For freedom, his life he gave.

Gave his all in a hell bent drive
One butchery morning in July,
Where three hundred and ten
Newfoundlanders did bravely die.

* *Battle of Beaumont Hamel.*

We Shall Remember Them
At Each Downing Of The Sun

Permission of the artist Brad Forward

*The Glorious Fruits of Victory
Were Won By Their Unselfish Sacrifice*

*Picture found in my
Great-grandparent's House
William and Catherine Noel*

Day Dreams

Photo by Frank Gogos

The Veteran Magazine

World War II

Photo by Peter Noel

166th Nlfd. Field Regiment, Royal Artillery gun, Royal Canadian Legion, Branch 56, St. John's, NL

My Daddy Was A Pilot
1957

My daddy was a pilot who answered to the call,
Went forth into battle, now I haven't a daddy at all.
Tonight here on my pillow, is a picture bright and true
Of my daddy's Spitfire as he heads her through the blue.

He flew with British fliers who won victory and fame
Flying the skies of England through fire shell and flame,
On an autumn evening with hundreds of planes in the air
Over the towers of London, where fliers knew no fear.

It was on this November night with the sky a battle hell
When struck by tracers his flaming fighter fell.
In peace he now is sleeping, in the town of Derbyshire
Where people still remember a young Newfoundland flier.

*This poem is dedicated to Thomas Ezra Clarke --
the very first poem I wrote while day dreaming in school.*

ASHBOURNE CEMETERY
Derbyshire, United Kingdom

Thomas Ezra Clarke was the son of Isaac and Mary Elizabeth Clarke of Freshwater. In 1941 he joined the Merchant Marines, but when he reached the shores of England he enlisted in the Royal Air Force. He attained the rank of Aircraftsman 1st Class. He was assigned to the 42nd Operational Training Unit until his death on November 7, 1942 at the age of 26.

He is buried in a Civilian Cemetery in Ashbourne, Derbyshire, United Kingdom.

Charles Davis Noel
At the gravestone of

THOMAS EZRA CLARKE

ASHBOURNE CEMETERY
Derbyshire, United Kingdom

Photos by Valerie Noel

Charles Davis was 23 years old when he died June 19, 1941 when his aircraft went down over the cliffs of Dover, England. He was the youngest son of George William and Fanny Mary (Noel) Davis of Freshwater. As a young boy growing up in Freshwater I would visit his parents on my way home from school. It was the custom of most young people in those days to visit the older residents of the community to lend a helping hand running errands, bringing water, or making kindling so they could quickly made a fire in the wood stoves on the cold winter mornings.

It was during these visits I got the inspiration to write Her Airman is Down.

Photo courtesy of Charles Davis Noel
Sgt. Charles Davis

UPPER HEYFORD CEMETERY
Oxfordshire, United Kingdom

© *Commonwealth War Graves Commission, UK*

Her Airman Is Down
1958

Her airman is down to fly no more
Along the coast of Newfoundland shore,
He gave his life so brave and true
As he flew in God's celestial blue,
He flew, he died, for what I ask,
To help make better this world of task?
He was a boy of twenty three - no more -
And died protecting the English shore,
Fighting for freedom, brave and bold,
His story shall not let go untold.
Though not an Englishman, I say,
He fought for England night and day.
He was a Newfoundlander, to me unknown,
Into God's blue, he'd bravely flown.
Why did he leave his friends and home
To fly up in that hysterical foam?
Why'd he leave his mother in dread,
Perhaps to hear one morning he is dead?
It was because he was a subject true,
He fought for the colors red, white and blue.

Here is his story as was told to me
How he went down protecting the free.

One day as he walked from school all alone
He learned of the courage the British had shown,
He heard at Dunkirk the British were trapped
Guns, machinery and men they lacked,
When suddenly he heard a great roar,
It was the R.C.A.F. going to England's shore.

Then on the radio this newsflash said,
"Hundreds of Brits are believed dead."
Then to his mother, eyes wild like fire,
Said ,"Oh Mom, oh Mom, my place is a flier,"
His mother turned with a quickened flash
"Yes, son," said she, "But your plane might crash,"
Then he saw a smile on his mother's face --
He knew when he left this would erase.
So forward he went to the English shore,
And fought through flame and battle roar.

Her airman was up and doing well,
But the rest of this story is sad to tell.
One night as his mother slept in her bed,
She dreamt that her boy flew overhead,
Saw her son as he flew with skill
Setting his course for a mighty kill.
Then she awakened with dreadful fright
For she dreamed a disastrous sight.
She saw his plane hurtling to earth,
Blood from his face ran down his shirt.
When she awoke all seemed clear,
But in passing hours, she filled with fear.

Then, as the evening sun went down,
All seemed quiet in the little town
When softly she heard a rap at the door,
Her heart skipped a beat as she crossed the floor
For there stood the Reverend silently, grave
Sadly, this is the message to her he gave.

YOUR SON, MISSING IN ACTION, BELIEVED KILLED.
HIS DUTY AND MISSION HE SUCCESSFULLY FULFILLED.

As she walked to his picture, eyes filled with tears
She thought of his triumphs, hopes and fears,

Of her airman down, who will fly no more,
Or dip his wings o'er Newfoundland shore,

Will walk no more life's path we tread,
Her thoughts were of a son now dead.
Then in the sky was a droning roar,
Aircraft returning from the English shore.
But, her airman is downed o'er cliffs of Dover
To forever sleep in a field of clover.

Charles Davis was a Newfoundlander. Newfoundland did not join Canada until 1949. During World War II many Newfoundlanders served in the British and Canadian forces.

Photo by Valerie Noel

Charles Davis Noel at the gravestone of Sgt. Charles Davis killed June 19, 1941 at the age of 23. His namesake Charles Davis Noel was born May 21, 1942.

World War II Lancaster Bomber

During WW II these planes were flown by both the British Royal Air Force and the Royal Canadian Air Force.

This poem is dedicated to all Canadians and Newfoundlanders who served in the Royal Canadian Air Force and the British Royal Air Force.

LAC Selby *Noel* enlisted in the RCAF in Sept. 1943 at St. John's. Newfoundland was not part of Canada until 1949, however the Canadian Air Force had a recruiting office in St. John's. He was selected to train as an Airo Engine Mechanic and trained in Ontario.

Photo courtesy of Elaine Noel
LAC Selby Noel

He first served at a Bombing & Gunnery Base in PEI and also later with the 124 Ferry Squadron, noted for its part in ferrying new aircraft overseas to the RAF. The bases at Gander and Goose Bay became very important as stopovers and refueling points for the operation. He held the rank of LAC (Leading Air Craftsman). He was late getting into the service. Newfoundland had no conscription so all who joined the forces were volunteers. After the war was over in Europe the RCAF was planning to send a unit to the Pacific to assist the US. He signed on and was on his way when the atomic bombs were used and the war ended. Discharged at Halifax in May 1946 he went home and used his benefits to further his education and graduated in 1951 with an Engineering degree. He worked with Canadian National Railways for 34 years at Moncton, St. John's, and Montreal. He retired in 1987 as System Equipment Engineer.

Forever Canada
1957

They flew in squadrons through the night
Flying onward, in their flight,
Flew with skill and oh, so high,
Sleep by day, at night would fly.

Flying bombers through hell and fire,
Their deeds and bravery we still admire,
Canada's men so brave and strong,
Fighting for right against wrong.

Fought like tigers protecting their young,
Answering calls when warnings were rung,
To protect mothers so true and dear,
They flew bombers through hostile air.

It was Canada's men in the air,
They fought with courage, without fear.
Flying their fighters away from home,
Protecting Ole England across the foam.

It was Canada's mother, Britain Great
Would she let her meet her fate?
Nay, Canada was a country, new,
To mother's aid on wings she flew.

Canada was not a country for war,
On the God of battles, sometimes swore.
When young men left friend and home
To fly up through that hell-made dome.

Many are missing, the stars only know,
To where on earth those men did flow,
It may be mountain, desert or sea,
But it will forever Canada be.

They Were Seven
1957

They were seven brothers
All sons of one mother
Who wisely taught all seven
To love and care for each other.

For years they lived happily
In a loving home together,
When bugles sounded war
All seven left their mother.

Three took khaki and the gun,
Two sailed on ocean's brow,
Two flew on wings in the air.
Where are those brothers now?

One lies somewhere in Italy,
In a valley green and low,
Above his sleeping head
Is a mountain capped with snow.

Two lie on beaches in Dieppe
For they are silent now,
And o'er their sandy graves
Cool ocean breezes blow.

Two have a watery grave
In surging waters deep,
Somewhere in mid-Atlantic,
Out where trade winds sweep.

There was one came to earth
Somewhere in a flaming "kite",
It seems God now only knows,
Where he made his final flight.

One sleeps in a field in Dover
With its cliffs of granite white,
It was here he joined his brothers
When he crashed one stormy night.

Yes, they were seven brothers,
All brave sons of one mother,
When bugles sounded war
All seven left home together.

May I ask this request of God?
For those boys were one in seven,
Give them a home sweet home,
And your eternal peace in heaven.

© *Commonwealth War Graves Commission, UK*
Suda Bay War Cemetery, Greece

Freshwater's Fallen Heroes WW I

Compiled from Commonwealth War Graves Commission, UK & Veterans Affairs, Canada

Private WALTER AUGUSTUS DEAN
Son of Matthew & Rhoda Dean,
* Great Brahat, White Bay
Died age 30 - October 25, 1918

*Address given when enlisted - Freshwater, Bay de Verde.

Private SIDNEY HARTTREE
First Battalion, Newfoundland Regiment
Son of Thomas & Mary Ann Harttree
Swansea, South Wales
Died age 23 - August 3, 1916

© Commonwealth War Graves Commission, UK
VICHTE MILITARY CEMETERY, Belgium

© Commonwealth War Graves Commission, UK
LIJSSENTHOEK MILITARY CEMETERY, Belgium

Message from the Minister of Militia: No. 949 Pt. Walter Dean killed in action. Please inform his next of kin (sister) Mrs. Elizabeth Sommers of Blow Me Down. (Freshwater Recorder, Vol. 1, June 1919, No. 10)

Sidney Harttree's parents lived in England but he lived with his brothers in Newark, New Jersey. He joined the Newfoundland Regiment on September 13, 1917 at St. John's. I do not know his connection to Freshwater, but he is mentioned in the Freshwater Recorder, Vol. 1, June 1919, No. 10, as being killed in action. It is possible he could have had friends or relatives living in the area.

Private SILAS JEFFERS
1st Battalion Royal Newfoundland Regiment
Son of Francis & Sarah Jeffers,
Freshwater, Bay de Verde
Died age 23 - July 1, 1916
Y RAVINE CEMETERY
Somme, France

Lance Corporal
SAMUEL J. MOORES
Killed in action - Battle of the Somme
Freshwater, Bay de Verde
Autumn 1916
UNKNOWN GRAVE*

Ordinary Seaman
FREDERICK J. (Fred) BUTT
H.M. Trawler, Othello II,
Newfoundland Royal Naval Reserve
Freshwater, Bay de Verde
Died age 20 - October 31, 1915
DOVER (ST. JAMES) CEMETERY

His body was never recovered. His name is displayed on the Beaumont Hamel Monument Memorial which contains the names of soldiers who have no known graves

*See Page 8

Freshwater's Fallen Heroes WW II

Compiled from Commonwealth War Graves Commission, UK & Veterans Affairs, Canada

Sergeant
CHARLES WILLIAM DAVIS
Royal Canadian Air Force
Died age 23 - June 19, 1941
Son of George E. & Fanny May Davis
Freshwater, Carbonear
UPPER HEYFORD CEMETERY
Oxfordshire, United Kingdom

Aircraftsman 1st Class
THOMAS EZRA CLARKE
Royal Air Force
42 Operational Training Unit
Son of Isaac & Mary Elizabeth Clarke,
Died age 26 - November 7, 1942
Freshwater, Carbonear
ASHBOURNE CEMETERY
Derbyshire, United Kingdom

Ordinary Seaman
GEORGE DOUGLAS PIKE
H.M.S. Palomares, Royal Navy
Died age 33 - November 9, 1942
Son of Douglas & Sophia Pike
Freshwater, Carbonear

Photo courtesy of Herbert Davis

Ordinary Seaman
HERBERT ALSTON DAVIS
HMS Avalon, Royal Navy
Died age 21 - October 20, 1943
Son of John Charles & Mary Ann Davis
Freshwater, Carbonear

Photo by Gee Noel Dwyer

UNITED CHURCH CEMETERY
Freshwater
When war broke out Herbert joined the British Royal Navy, Att. HMCS Avalon. While home on leave he died of tuberculosis.

Freshwater Citizens Who Served

Compiled from Commonwealth War Graves Commission, UK
& Veterans Affairs, Canada

World War I

Newfoundland Royal Navy Reserve
Penney, Andrew Freeman
Butt, William Alfred
Parsons, William T.
Moores, Edward P.
Noel, George A.
Butt, Nathaniel
Harvey, Hedley
Howell, James
Butt, Leander
Butt, Frederick J.

Ist Bn Royal Newfoundland Regiment
Pte. Dean, Walter (Blow Me Down)
Lcpl. Moores, Samuel
Pte. Harttree, Sidney
Pte. Jeffers, Silas

Royal Newfoundland Regiment
Rev. Sgt. Parsons, John W.
Soper, George Plemon
Barrett, Eugene
Howell, Malcolm

Canadian Army
Rev. Cpl. Davis, Chas. F. M.S.M
Sgt. Davis, John Shenstone
Butt, William Alfred
Moores, Ernest
Callahan, John

United States Army
Sgt. Joyce, Thomas Lloyd

World War II

Royal Navy
AB. Pike, George Douglas
OS. Davis, Herbert Alston
AB. Davis, Norman Warren
AB. Noel, Reuben James
AB. Harvey, Nicholas

Royal Canadian Navy
Sub Lt. Noel, George Stanley

Wrens
Priddle, Beatrice (Evely) (Flatrock)

Merchant Navy
Butt, George (also N.O.F.U.)
Noel, George Benjamin
Noel, Richard
Clarke, Thomas Ezra (also RAF)

**166th Nfld. Field Regiment
Royal Artillery**
Sgt. Maj. Parsons, Charles Clayton
Gnr. Moores, Roy Clifford
Bdr. Noel, William LeRoy

**59th Nfld. Heavy Regiment
Royal Artillery**
Sgt. Clarke, Frederick Allen

Newfoundland Regiment
Cpl. Butt, Roland James
Cpl. Davis, William Harrison
Cpl. Harvey, Charles J.
Cpl. Davis, Clifford

Royal Canadian Army
Pte. Janes, Raleigh Lester
[PPCLI] E101401
Pte. Harvey, James

RCA Medical Corps
Capt. Pottle, Clarence Herbert (Flatrock)

Royal Canadian Army CWAC
Pte. Butt, Mary Ann

Royal Air Force
ACJ. Clarke, Thomas Ezra
LAC. Butt, Clarence Reginald
W/O. Moores, Samuel Angus

Royal Canadian Air Force
F/Sgt. Parsons, Joseph T. Horwood
Sgt. Davis, Charles William
LAC. Noel, Selby

WAFS
LAW. McIntyre, Jean Winnifred (Bowers)
LAW Pye, Melvina (Butt)

Newfoundland Overseas Forestry Unit
Mullins, Francis (Frank)
Parsons, Maxwell
Ash, William R.
Harvey, Roy

Vietnam War
United States Air Force
Sgt. Noel, Roland L. SAC/AAC

Peace Keepers

Royal Canadian Air Force
W/O Thoms, Garrett (Garry)
Cpl. Glenda (Butt) Trepanier
Maj. Parsons, Yvonne

Royal Canadian Navy
AB Noel, Dale

Royal Canadian Army
M/Cpl. Evely, Raymond (Flatrock)
Cpl. Pottle, Eric (Flatrock)
Pte. Parsons, Dwayne
Cpl. Butt, Kevin (Bud)
Pte. Butt, Benjamin

Canadian Army Reserves
M/Cpl. Noel, Beverly
Cpl. Snow, Dale

Afghanistan War

Canadian Army
C/WO Parsons, Lindsey
W/O Parsons, Robert
M/Cpl. Noel, Crystal
Cpl. Hiscock, Adam
Ptv. Parsons, Kent
Pte. Davis, Carson
M/Cpl. Noel, Scott
Parsons, Darrell
W/O Snow, Jason
W/O Snow, Scott
Davis, Brian

Canadian Navy
LT/CDR Noel, Michael
P/O 1st Murphy, Davis
Davis, Austin

PORTSMOUTH NAVAL MEMORIAL

© Commonwealth War Gravess Commisssion, UK

After the First World War, the Naval Memorial was created to commemorate those members of the Royal Navy who had no known grave, the majority of deaths having occurred at sea where no permanent memorial could be provided.

A/B George Douglas Pike

© *Veterans Affairs, Canada*
A/B George Douglas Pike

When World War II broke out he joined the British Royal Navy and served on the HMS Palomares. He died November 9, 1942, age 33. His name is inscribed on Panel 72, Column 2, Portsmouth Naval Memorial, Portsmouth Sound, England.

In November 1942, HMS Palomares took part in the Operation Torch landings in Algiers as an Anti Aircraft ship. The ship left Gibraltar on the 3rd, arriving on the 8th. The next day the HMS Palomares was hit by a bomb, suffering a large number of casualties.

HMS Palomares - August 1941

FL 1284 © IWM   *Imperial War Museum, UK*

Psalm 107:23-31

They that go down to the sea in ships, that do business in great waters,
These see the works of the Lord, and His wonders in the deep.
For He commandeth, and raiseth the stormy wind, which lifteth up the waves thereof.
They mount up to the heaven, they go down again to the depths; their soul is melted because of trouble.
They reel to and fro, and stagger like a drunken man, and are at their wits' end.
Then they cry out unto the Lord in their trouble, and He bringeth them out of their distresses.
He maketh the storm a calm, so that the waves thereof are still.
Then they are glad because they be quiet; so He bringeth them unto their desired haven.
Oh that men would praise the Lord for His goodness, and for His wonderful works to the children of men!

The Holy Bible
King James Version

Forget-Us-Not
April 26, 1959

We the dead, forget us not,
We faced a morning blazing sun,
Now lie in a red stained plot
Where a nation's blood did run.

We scrambled to meet the throng
Fell, and died by The Danger Tree
Defending right, defeating wrong.
Our lives we gave, and gave it free.

Pick up the torch from out our wake
Raise it high for freedom's sake.

Forget - Forget - Forget us not.
Look o'er stones that mark our plot
And wear for us a Forget - Me - Not.

Created by Dennis Flanders

FOR OUR FREEDOM THEY GAVE THEIR ALL
Forget - Them - Not

Christmas Peace
December 1963

Once again it is Christmas time and the world seems all alight,
From its dawn of bitter quarreling, that follows a hostile night.
Christmas is the time, my friends, when past things are forgot,
So with the coming New Year, let us tie the friendship knot.

Let past feuds be forgotten, let the future come anew,
Let the world with its many peoples find a place for me and you,
That we may live in liberty and walk life's road together,
And live in a world community where man is to each a brother.

Peace on earth be our motto, as in the days of long ago,
When wise men and shepherds saw the light o'er a manger glow,
May we know no more of turmoil, endless care and strife
But good will towards our fellow man, in this our earthly life.

Pray this will be the Christmas the world will see the light,
And its nations with the closing eve make for us a peaceful night,
That our guns will never echo through the future hills of time,
That we may live in unison where echoing peace bells chime.

Bdr. William LeRoy Noel

166th Nfld. Field Regiment
Royal Artillery
December 28, 1942
Waterford, England

I wrote this poem in 1963 while awaiting orders to report to Lackland Air Force Base in San Antonio, Texas to begin my basic training in the USAF.

I dedicate this poem to William LeRoy Noel, who served in World War II with the 166th Newfoundland Field Regiment, Royal Artillery attached to the British 8th Army.

The 166th fought in North Africa and Italy and saw heavy combat at the Battle of Monte Cassino. This was the Regiment's finest hour for it was here not only did they fight the enemy, but also the mountainous terrain, and winter and spring's merciless elements.

The Battle Of Monte Cassino

NA 15141 © IWM   Imperial War Museum, UK

B9985 © IWM   Imperial War Museum, UK

Destruction of the Benedictine Monastery

The Battle of Monte Cassino was one of the largest and bloodiest fought in Europe during World War II. Here the 166th Newfoundland Field Regiment (Royal Artillery) assignment was to give artillery support to infantry regiments and units from the many different countries which were engaged in the battle. British Command also used the 166th Regiment extensively during shelling of the Benedictine Monastery that stood on a very high hill overlooking the town of Monte Cassino and which the German Army had heavily fortified.

The Regiment also saw action in North Africa. Its batteries were actively engaged on the Tunisian front giving artillery support to the French and British units until the end of the campaign.

Throughout the British 8th Army, Gunners of the 166th were known for their versatility, accuracy, high angle trajectory and rapid fire and were often compared to army sharp shooters. They were also called the "Roving Regiment", and "five mile or long distance snipers".

Freshwater gunners taking part in the battle:
Gnr. Roy Clifford Moores
Bdr. William LeRoy Noel

25-pounders of the 430th Battery, 55th Field Regiment, near Hechtel in Belgium, firing in support of Guards Armoured Division in the bridgehead over the Maas-Schelde.

25 Pounder Field Guns used by the British and Commonwealth Countries including the 166th Newfoundland Field Regiment (Royal Artillery) at Monte Cassino.

166th Hat Badge

Photo courtesy of Leslie Noel Foward

Photo courtesy of son David Parsons

Sgt/Maj. Charles Clayton Parsons
1913 - 1977
Son of
Stephen & Sarah (Davis) Parsons

Prior to WW II, Clayton was a member of the Royal Nfld. Constabulary. He served with the 166th Nfld. Field Regiment in North Africa and Italy, achieving the rank of Sergeant Major. After the war, he joined the Royal Canadian Mounted Police (RCMP), and in 1962 started the family business M.A. Parsons Ltd.

The 59th Nfld. Heavy Regiment (Royal Artillery)
Training in England

D 8888 © IWM

Imperial War Museum, UK

Sgt. Frederick Allan Clarke
Freshwater Gunner

The 59th Regiment was active after the Normandy invasion giving artillery support to the second Canadian Division in their attacks on Falaise and Montigny.

In September 1944, the 59th was in action at Nijmegen supporting the airborne landing at Arnhem.

Their final operations were in the British sector of the Western front with the capture of Bremen and the crossing of the Elbe at Lauenburg, Germany.

©Photo by Don Tate, Newfoundland Grand Banks Genealogy Site

Newfoundland Militia

Photo courtesy of wife Lillian
Cpl. Roland James Butt

September 1939. With the onset of World War II the Commission Government decided to establish a home defense force. In October, it created the Newfoundland Militia, later renamed the Newfoundland Regiment in 1943. Before hostilities ended, the Regiment had enlisted some 1,668 men, whose mission was to guard vulnerable areas in St. John's, Bell Island, Harbour Grace, Bay Roberts, Whitbourne, and St. Lawrence. The 166th Newfoundland Field Regiment (Royal Artillery) and 59th Newfoundland Heavy Regiment (Royal Artillery) also received recruits from this regiment. Other Freshwater members of the Newfoundland Militia: Cpl. William Harrison Davis, Cpl. Charles J., Harvey, and Cpl. Clifford Davis.

The Newfoundland Overseas Forestry

Photo courtesy of daughter Sylvia Parsons Pelley
Maxwell Parsons
Maxwell was a member of the N.O.F.U. and also the home guard in Scotland.

At the outbreak of WW II the Government of Newfoundland sent 3,600 loggers overseas. These volunteers formed the Newfoundland Overseas Forestry Unit (N.O.F.U.) to supply timber products critical to British coal mining operations. The first draft of 350 men sailed from St. John's to Liverpool on December 13, 1939. By mid-February, the entire unit had arrived in Britain and worked in forests from southern England to the Scottish Highlands, making them the first Newfoundlanders to enter the war.

Other Freshwater members:
Francis (Frank) Mullins & Roy Harvey

Newfoundland Forestry Corps working in forests of Scotland, ca. 1917. ©

Merchant Marines

During the Second World War, the Merchant Marines played a vital role. They were the sailors who transported desperately needed food, equipment, and fuel to Britain and other Allied countries on non-military vessels.

They were not part of the Navy: they were civilians -- men and women who faced constant threat from the enemy and the sea. Thousands lost their lives and hundreds of others were captured and sent to prisoner of war camps. Many never returned home.

Their ships were lightly armed and sailed in convoys, escorted by warships and aircraft of many countries, but they were still at risk of enemy planes and submarines, especially German U-boats.

Freshwater Merchant Marines:
George Butt (also N.O.F.U), George Benjamin Noel, & Richard Noel

© RAF - PC 71/19/591   *Royal Air Force Museum, UK*

Merchant ships steaming in convoy. Oblique aerial view with the wingtip float of a Sunderland in the top left.

D-Day Landing June 6, 1944

Photo courtesy of his daughter
Barbara Noel Drover
Reuben Noel

A/B Reuben James Noel

During World War II he served with the British Royal Navy in both the Atlantic and the Pacific. On D-Day he was a British LCA driver similar to the photo (below left) of the Canadian LCA, ferrying British and Allied forces to and from the war-torn beaches.

After the war he returned home and served with the Newfoundland Rangers and the Royal Canadian Mounted Police.

© Library and Archives Canada

LCA (Landing Craft Assault) form line ahead as they move off from the landing ship Langby Castle, carrying troops of the Winnipeg Rifles to Juno Beach, Normandy June 6, 1944.

Photo courtesy of Barbara Noel Drover
George Stanley Noel

Lt. George Noel, *brother* of Reuben Noel, *served as a lieutenant in the Royal Canadian Navy on a submarine during World War II. According to his niece, Barbara, George met his wife, Chrissie, at the Newfoundland Club in the basement of St. Martin's in the Fields, Trafalgar Square, which is now a coffee house.*

© Photo by Robert Thornhill   *Courtesy of Thornhill Photography*

http://www.robertthornhillphotography.ca

Nicholas (Nick) Noel
(wearing his great-grandfather's World War II uniform)

Hannah Dwyer
(dressed as an army nurse)
Author of "A Day To Remember" page 50

LAST SALUTE
November 11, 1997

Photo courtesy of Leslie Noel Forward

Front Row: Wm. LeRoy Noel, CD, Art Reid – MHA Carbonear District.
Back Row: Mayor Claude Garland, Bugler Brett Pilgrim – 589 Carbonear Air Cadet Sqd., Deputy Mayor Sam Slade, Gilbert Noel.

William LeRoy Noel, *a veteran of World War II and the Battle of Monte Cassino was a speaker that day. The next morning he had a severe heart attack and died November 13, 1997. This would be his last salute.*

*Old soldiers, sailors and airmen never die,
they just march and sail and fly out into eternity.*

CARBONEAR WAR MEMORIAL
November 11, 2008

ALL GAVE SOME
SOME GAVE ALL

The phrase, "All gave some; some gave all," is widely attributed to the Korean War veteran and Purple Heart recipient Howard William Osterkamp from Dent, Ohio. Osterkamp served in the US Army from 1951 to 1953.

A Day To Remember
© Hannah Dwyer
2008

The sun set on the Battle Field,
The end of yet another day.
Soldiers, tired and wounded,
On their bunks, they lay.

The morning horn had sounded.
The soldiers strong and brave,
Marched into battle,
Fearless of early graves.

Fighting for their families,
Countries and freedom, too.
Even though the doctors tried,
There was nothing they could do.

Each dead soldier's body was buried,
Then labelled with a cross.
To remember where they'd buried,
Each tragic and sorrowful loss.

Today when we remember,
A few minutes we shall spend.
But, the question really is,
Will war ever really end?

Cherish Your Freedoms
- Paid For In Full -
With Blood, Sweat and Tears
****
Let No Person Take It From You

A Thanks To Those Who Serve Keeping Us Safe Each Day

Photo by Derm Chafe

Const. Beverley Noel, RCMP, saluting the flag on Remembrance Day.

A Tribute To My American Friends

© US Navy - 80-G-464654   US Naval History & Heritage Command

Convoy WS-12 Vought SB2U scout bomber from USS Ranger (CV-4) flies anti-submarine patrol over the convoy, while it was enroute to Cape Town, South Africa,

Seamen First Class
Walter Joyce
Photo courtesy of daughter Serena Joyce

Born in Chelsea, Massachusetts, son of Joseph and Gertrude (Noel) Joyce, both formerly of Freshwater. He entered the United States Navy as a seaman first class on April 30, 1945. After basic training in New York, he was stationed on board the USS Adirondack flagship in Norfolk, Virginia. Walter was the Captain's skiff (small boat) driver, and because he played the cornet and guitar he was present to perform when the captain entertained other officers. The USS Adirondack received her commission the day the war officially ended. He drove the Captain to the ship on which the peace treaty was signed. He was honorably discharged on March 20, 1946.

Seaman First Class
Larry Noel
Photo courtesy of granddaughter
Bonnie Noel Mousney

Born in Revere, Massachusetts, son of Stanley (from Freshwater) and Mae Squib (from Carbonear) Noel. He enlisted in the United States Navy during World War II and served in the Atlantic and the Pacific. When on watch at Kodiak Island, Alaska, his eyeball froze. He returned to the Lower Forty-eight for treatment. At one point Larry and his brother Raymond were in the same convoy crossing the Atlantic, but on different ships. For a time he was stationed at the US Naval Station in Argentia, Newfoundland. After the war, he received an honorable discharge from the Navy.

M/Sgt. Robert (Jim) Russell
Photo courtesy of daughter
Bonnie Russell Gillette

Born in Lawrence County, Ohio, son of Henry and Sadie Russell. At a young age, he enlisted as an infantryman in the US Army in World War II. In the European Theater at the age of seventeen, he saw heavy combat as the US Army pushed their way into Germany. Five years later, he again found himself in combat in the Korean War. Here he received the Purple Heart. He switched services when the war was over and joined the United States Air Force. In the 1950s, while stationed in St. John's, Newfoundland, he met Hope Christopher of Port-de-Grave and they married in Port-de-Grave in 1958. Again, during the Vietnam War he received further deployment to Vietnam. He told his superiors he would prefer not to go to war a third time. They honored his request. He served his country in military service for twenty-seven years.

Private First Class
John H. Mercer

Born in Bay Roberts, Newfoundland, June 15, 1921, son of John and Ethel Spencer Mercer. John joined the United States Army in August 1942. He was assigned to the 100th Infantry Division. This unit fought their way through France and Germany. Along the way they were engaged in heavy combat and suffered huge losses. Their longest and hardest fought battles were at Alsace-Lorraine and Bitche in France. As part of General Patton's 7th Army, the Division was ordered to halt the attack and to hold defensive positions south of Bitche as part of its mission leading up to the Battle of the Bulge.

One Man's Story

I meet Samuel Bernstein when attending a Masonic meeting at Major General Henry Knox Military Lodge located in Boston. As one of the few living survivors of the Battle of Iwo Jima, he was being honored for his service

World War II Honoree

World War II Veteran

Samuel 'Sammy' Bernstein

BRANCH OF SERVICE
U.S. Marine Corps

HOMETOWN
New London, CT

HONORED BY
Roberta Bernstein, Wife

ACTIVITY DURING WWII
SERVED AS CAMOUFLAGE INSTRUCTOR AT CAMP PENDLETON. LANDED IN THE 5TH WAVE ON IWO JIMA AND FOUGHT IN LAST BANZAI AND THE OCCUPATION OF JAPAN. MEMBER OF COMPANY A, 5TH PIONEER BATTALION, 5TH MARINE DIVISION.

April 11, 1924 - Dec 27, 2015

March 7, 1945 at Iwo Jima

<u>Sammy's Story</u>

On March 7th I was at the cemetery with a chaplain where I was one of his assistants when he needed help. We were burying two of our boys. I was very upset. I sat down to write a letter to my mother and father to tell them what I was seeing and would hope to maybe send it to them if I could. An officer bent over me and asked if he could be of any help. I told him of the letter and he said he was flying to Guam that day and and if I gave him my folks' address he would send it to them. A year later when I got home my folks showed me the mail from marine headquarters that came from me. It was my poem.

Oh, I Just Saw A Sight

Pfc. Samuel Bernstein
March 7, 1945

Oh, I just saw a sight to see,
A sight that will always live with me,
And there they were row on row,
The graves of boys who gave their all.

Here a cross and there a star,
Try to see it 'cause here they are,
A Catholic, Protestant, and a Jew,
All American boys we once knew.

And though you read, "so many thousand dead"
You know not what you really read
'Cause only these who see their graves
Will ever know and be amazed.

So to the ones who must receive
A notice that they've been bereaved,
The boys they died for four great rights*,
We alive, for all time, must keep them bright.

And when it's over, God make it soon,
Lest we forget 'ere we're doomed,
That war is hell and pray we must
To keep the peace they gave to us.

© *Written on March 7th, 1945 at Iwo Jima at the 5th Marine Division Cemetery.*

* *Freedom of speech, Freedom of worship, Freedom from want, Freedom from fear*

Dedicated To All Canadians

Photo by Jim Arpan

Who Served In The United States Military During the Vietnam War 1960 - 1975

Canada as a country was not involved in the Vietnam War, but according to some accounts there were 35,000 to 40,000 Canadian citizens who served in the United States military during the war. About 12,000 served in Vietnam. There were 113 killed, and 7 missing in action. Their names are on the Vietnam Memorial Wall in Washington D.C. and on Canada's Vietnam memorial called the North Wall Monument located in Assumption Park, Windsor, Ontario, overlooking the Detroit River.

As in the US, many Canadians who served in Vietnam returned home to despicable treatment. This was especially noticeable in Toronto and Vancouver where US draft dodgers had settled. These large cities were often the site of anti-war hostility.

WE THE PEOPLE SALUTE YOU

Massena, Iowa military recognition stone.

The North Wall Park

Photos by Jim Arpan

Through the lonely night of silence

MAC - C141 Starlifter - Military Airlift Command, USAF
Photo Public Domain

Sgt. Roland L. Noel
USAF 1964 - 1970

It was 1967, Elmendorf Air Force Base, Alaska. My roommate and I were heading to Michigan to spend Thanksgiving with his family. We hitched a ride on a MAC C141 Starlifter Aircraft that had landed to refuel on a return flight from Vietnam.

Our exuberance knew no bounds as we boarded. To our surprise, the aircraft was almost full of Navy Seabees. They still had mud on their boots and looked forlorn, quiet and tired. The crew chief pointed to the rear of the aircraft where there were several flag-draped coffins and gave us instructions.

I dedicate this poem to those fallen heroes with whom I flew on that flight. It was written one night after reflecting on my time in the service. It was a very sobering experience for us young airmen at the time. I can still hear the silence and the whine of the engines. It was a long flight home.

The Long Flight Home
February 16, 2011

I boarded a flight in Elmendorf,
With others who were granted leave,
We were heading to the forty-eight,*
To enjoy a Thanksgiving Eve.

As we headed up the stairway,
We were making an awful noise,
For we were heading homeward
To share in turkey joys.

When clambering to our seats,
As we readied for the ride,
The crew chief came toward us
Saying, "Yesterday, comrades died".

He pressed his finger against his lips,
And then to the cargo door,
Where we saw the flag draped coffins,
Then heard the engines roar.

He came along, and whispered
To each airman, one on one,
Saying, "On this flight, young men
There are tasks that must be done.

You will not move! You will sit, there!
As reverently as if in church today,
You stand there at attention
When the honor guard pass your way.

Here you sit with honoured men,
God's brave chosen few
Who are wearing Army green,
Navy and Air Force blue."

Through the lonely night of silence,
With the engines whining roar,
The honour guard stood standing
By the flag draped coffins' door.

The flight moving ever forward
Through freezing midnight air,
Bringing them ever, ever closer
To families who loved them dear.

As dawn's new day was breaking
Through the haze of an Eastern sky,
Each one of us was thinking,
There but for the grace of God go I.**

Soon we heard engines slowing,
As we approached the soil below
Then saw the tower's beacon,
With its guiding lights aglow.

We felt the aircraft dip its wings
When moving left to right,
Heard the captain answer, "Roger
I have your glide path in our sight.

MAC to tower, this is Starlifter one four one.
Turning right on final -- code name Uncle Sam --
Bringing home our fallen heroes
From blood soaked fields of 'Nam'.

---

* *Lower forty-eight in Alaska refers to the forty-eight states below the 49th parallel that runs between Canada and the United States.*

***No one is quite sure who coined the phrase. This expression has been attributed to John Bradford (1510 - 1555) who so remarked on seeing criminals being led to their execution. There is no written record of him ever using this phase. A number of religious leaders, including John Bunyan, have been credited with it as well. In addition, Winston Churchill is on record as using the phrase.*

C-141 Touch Down

Photo by Jeff Fisher   National Museum of the U.S. Air Force

C-141 touch down at the National Museum of the U.S. Air Force during its final flight on May 6, 2006.

For more than 40 years, The C-141s performed numerous airlift missions for the USAF. With its great range and high speed, the Starlifter projected American military power and humanitarian efforts rapidly across the globe.

The C-141 was the aircraft used by the Military Airlift Command, USAF to move men and material to and from Vietnam. It was on such an aircraft, on a November night in 1967 I made the long flight home with a group of United States Navy Seabees along with wounded and dead servicemen returning to the United States.

> **NOT *EVERYONE WHO LOST HIS LIFE IN VIETNAM DIED THERE, NOT EVERYONE WHO CAME HOME FROM VIETNAM EVER LEFT THERE***

Engraved on a stone at the Vietnam War Memorial in Odessa, TX

I wrote this poem based on a true experience told to me by a marine, Paul Smith, from the fields of Vietnam. I admit when writing this poem I took advantage of poetic license and inserted my own feelings on the Vietnam War and how those young servicemen were treated by their politicians and public at large. I dedicate this poem to his memory. Paul served two tours of duty with the U.S. Marines in Vietnam and received two Purple Hearts. Like many other combat soldiers who witnessed the horrors of war, it took a toll on him and he died at an early age.

Troops On The Ground In Vietnam

© 530610   National Archives and Records Administration, USA

PFC Paul F. Smith

They Served Their Country

Fought A War

Returned Home

To An Ungrateful Uncle Sam.

A Marine From The Fields Of Vietnam
March 3, 2011

He and I walked along a winding wooded path,
I noticed his shoulders, moving left and right,
As a helicopter hovered, passing in our view,
I asked, "Why?" he said, "It often comes to sight."

When I hear a chopper, it carries me back to 'Nam
I often flash back to a day on a jungle trail,
When a sergeant and I were crossing over a gully bridge,
and looked in silent horror as we leaned upon its rail.

For on the other side, was a sight beyond one's fear.
We saw young children with grenades in hand.
With our weapons drawn and pulses running fast,
We stood transfixed in that war-torn jungle land.

The children ran toward us, waving hands in air,
Question came to mind, had they pulled the safety pin.
Then as they approached us within a yard or two
From their little hands, grenades did wildly spin.

As the grenades were falling just beyond our feet,
Children all went screaming down a dusty road
The two of us went leaping into a watery ditch
There we waited for the grenades to explode.

Finally, we found courage to inspect those balls of death
And to our disbelief, found the pins were all intact,
Then we heard the pop of engines from choppers overhead
And watched them break formation, readied for an attack.

We stood in frozen terror awaiting a battle storm,
When to our surprise saw circling choppers land.

Villagers come running toward those whirlybirds
On this eerie morning, the village would disband.

The Night before, the Cong* came destroying crops and farm
Now they lived in horror, they said they would return
Someone in your village is aiding South Vietnam.
If you do not ID him, you will see homes and family burn.

Whenever I hear a chopper, it drifts me back to 'Nam**
I get an old time feeling to shift my shoulders left to right,
As it was my custom when hitting the fields in Vietnam -
Yes! Still I see these children in haunting dreams at night.

There are many untold stories of the fighting men in 'Nam,
He said, "A bloody nightmare for soldiers on the ground,
While cowardly politicians, got votes written with our blood,
As war-dodging hippie protesters were degrading us abound".

"We did the best we could, in those years of discontent,
When draft dodging hippies, refusing to join the war,
Convinced hypocrite politicians, not to fund us in our fight,
Leaving us defenseless like we were scumbags at their door."

With those words, returned to the place from whence we came.
Never again to mention the lost years he spent in Vietnam.
He was among the many that fought a winless, bloodied war
Only to return home in silence, to an ungrateful Uncle Sam.

Paul was my friend and co-worker, and often on our lunch break we would take a walk through the park. One day as we walked, a helicopter flew low overhead and I saw him hunker down and shift his shoulders left and right. I asked him why and he said, "It takes me back to my days in Vietnam. Whenever I'd jump from a chopper I would adjust my backpack as I hit the drop zone".

A few nights later after a few drinks of scotch, he told me a story of how he and his sergeant were walking a jungle trail when they came upon some young children playing with hand grenades. He said, "We both stopped and pulled our weapons as the children approached." He looked me straight in the eye and asked, "What would you do?" then dropped his eyes to the glass. I took a sip and let the question go unanswered. After a long pause in a low soft voice he said, "No casualties, the pins weren't pulled." We never again spoke of the war. This one event left a haunting impression on Paul.

*Cong - GI slang for North Vietnamese soldiers

**Nam - GI slang for Vietnam

Arlington National Cemetery
Memorial Day 2008

Photo in Public Domain
Wikimedia Commons, free media repository

SOLDIERS' MONUMENT
Washington, D.C.

Photo by Justin Noel

THE VIETNAM WALL MEMORIAL
Washington, D.C.

Photo by Justin Noel

The Salvation Army
Serving Young Sailors - Soldiers - Airmen

19730004-13 © CWM   Canadian War Museum

From a day in France, 1917 when a Salvation Army woman handed a fresh doughnut to a young soldier, they became known to the troops as the "Salvation Army lassies." They were also called the "doughnut girls."

The Young Soldiers
1963

Oh come you young soldiers who fight for the Lord,
Come let us all join in with one great accord,
Link our young voices that we might be heard,
As we march forth in glory with God's living word.

There are times in this world of struggle and strife,
When man is all self and gives nothing of life,
Yet, we the young soldiers of salvation might,
We will guide the lost sinner to God's glowing light.

For God is our captain up there in the sky,
He watches our movements as we march by.
So let us keep in step as we march along
As we fight the good fight, to crush the foes' wrong.

The blood and the fire is our lone bugle's call
While our drums are rolling, the foe we will stall,
Tho' our banners be lowered or our flag flying high
Redemption of sin is our one charging cry.

Oh faith be our shield and the Bible our sword,
We will fight the good fight in the name of our Lord,
So come you young soldiers of salvation might
As we march on to victory by day and by night.

For we the young warriors in the crusade of God
Shall fight manfully onward both home and abroad,
When our drums are rolling to that final call,
God will be our fortress until the last of us fall.

I wrote this poem after attending Sunday services at the Salvation Army in Chelsea, Massachusetts.

"A MONTH Of REMEMBRANCE"
PRAY FOR PEACE
Roland L. Noel

November 11th is a day long remembered in the hearts and minds of men. For it was on the eleventh hour, the eleventh day, the eleventh month, that the first great global war came to a close.

It is upon this day each year that around the free nations of the world men and women will stand at war memorials and lift their hearts in prayer and remembrance. Around the world, flags will fly and bands will play, and as the sun sinks slowly down the cold autumn sky, in the distant shadows of eventide one may hear the bugler sound The Last Post of his comrade who has fought and died in freedom's name.

Somewhere on a rock bound coast, as the ocean billows roll, one may see a misty-eyed mother as she stares across the water; and in her visions, she sees her son on the crest of every wave as he sets his course for the low grey horizon beyond to fight and die, so man might be free.

Then, as we look across the waters to some other shore, one might see a father who also remembers a son or daughter as he or she once stood in the autumn shadows of crimson and gold and bid farewell to home, friends and country to march away into the distance to sleep in foreign soil.

Then as the mighty cannons fire their memorial salute and the thundering jets sweep the skies in their fly pass, a son and daughter may raise their heads with pride and remembrance of a father who once thundered his aircraft down the sky lanes, dipped his wings and roared into the distance to return no more but to place his name on freedom's honoured roll call.

Yes, the sons and daughters of the free countries of the world have fought and died with gallantry around the world wherever our freedom has been threatened.

From the dawn of times creation, man has struggled to be free and today, we of the United States, stand justly proud of our country. It was only through the sweat, blood, toil and tears of the unselfish sacrifices of our sons and daughters who fought and died in the wars down through the years that today, this eleventh of November, we stand free.

But, as we remember them at the going down of the sun and The Last Post echoes in the distant mountains, as the flag is lowered to half-mast, we ask that you raise your heart in prayer and remember the sons and daughters who at this moment are paying the supreme sacrifice in the jungles of Vietnam. PRAY FOR PEACE that our men and women may come home to FIGHT NO MORE!

The Protestant Adult League of the chapel asks you to attend a church of your choice during November and give a special word of prayer for peace, and remember, "when a man's ways please the Lord, he maketh even his enemies to be at peace with him" (Proverbs 16:7). "Behold how good and how pleasant it is for brethren to dwell together in unity" (Psalms. 133:1).

Reprint of an article I wrote for the PAL News Letter when stationed at Elemendorf Air Force Base, Alaska.

Photo © 1996.253.7267.002   US Navy National Museum of Naval Aviation

The Old Veteran
February 1961

He was ragged and worn, aged with years,
Thought of his past, his hopes and fears,
A youth away from friends and home
In a foreign country, all alone.
Seeing men pass in elegant form,
No joy in his heart, he came to mourn.
Mourn for men that had gone before,
And will walk with him never more.
Thought of nights in muck and mire,
Days he pushed through hell's grit fire.
As bullets and shells flew low overhead,
Men in dugouts fell wet, cold and dead.
Long night marches in rain and flood,
With a burst of shells, boys grew to manhood.
He remembered days of hunger and cold
Where men of perception lost sense of soul.
He looked at his medals untarnished, with pride,
Glanced at his cane that stood by his side.
Looking around in his unruffled way,
Thought of comrades, where they lay.
The procession passed with a drummer's beat,
When bugles compounded, he stood to his feet.
With cane in hand, took praise worthy stride,
From a tear on his cheek, you know he cried.
Although he was old, feeble with age,
Toward the monument, proudly did page.
He took a salute, which no one can expound,
His lamented heart was felt abound.

Elemendorf AFB Anchorage, Alaska
Base Chapel

OFFICE OF THE
BASE CHAPLAIN
Elemendorf AFB
Alaska

19 March 1968

Dear Sergeant Noel

Congratulations on your winning entry in the Protestant Religious Writing Contest. Your prize was well deserved, and we thank you for your participation.

The Project Officer, Chaplain Keeney, informs me that the competition was keen and the standard of entries unusually high. May I urge you to continue to nurture your talent in the field of religious writing.

Again, my heartiest congratulations for an outstanding entry and, in the end, a winner.

Sincerely

VICTOR H. SCHROEDER, Ch, Col, USAF   1 Atch
Base Chaplain   Religious Writing Contest Entry

Mailing Address: ELCH — 21st Air Base Group, APO Seattle 98742

September 11, 2001

A Day of Shock

And

Disbelief

This Page is Dedicated To My Friend and Co-Worker
September 11, 2001

Photo courtesy of her mother Francine Kaplan

Robin Kaplan

My friend and co-worker, Robin Kaplan, together with six other TJX employees - Christine Barbuto, Nellie Casey, Tara Creamer, Linda George, Lisa Fenn Gordenstein and Susan MacKay - were on American Air Lines Flight 11, September 11, 2001 when it was hijacked and flown into the World Trade Center.

Day Dreams

A Place Called Home

The House On The Hill
Built 1915

Let me lie in my bed in that house on the hill
And wait for the sound of Santa Claus's bell.

Photo by Davis Noel

George and Gertrude Noel's House

Our Ancestors
October 20, 1981

I have stood within their footsteps, as I walked the valley low,
Heard the echo of their voices, through the drift of ice and snow,
Have felt their spirit present, as I left the harbour's shore,
Saw them in my vision, through the lightening thunder's roar.
Have smelt the distant ochre as they barked their nets and twine,
As they readied for the harvest of the sea at fishing time,
Saw them in the twilight, ride the wave of a raging storm,
And heard them singing praises on a blessed Sabbath morn.
For as their songs rebounded, in the valley and the dale
They only asked His guidance, through life's uncertain gale.

I have stood there on the headlands, thought far beyond my dreams,
Thought of where they came from -- no one cared it seems --
Heard their many stories, as through my boyhood passed
Yet from where did they come? the question still is asked.
Some say the Jersey Islands, others, old England grand.
The only thing that's certain is they came to Newfoundland.
Why they came to Newfoundland is far beyond my reach.
Yet I searched and searched to find it, as I crossed the rocky beach,
As I look towards the heavens, where the headlands meet the sky
I get that ever-haunting question, for what? and when? and why?

I have sailed upon their waters, in the chill of an autumn breeze,
Felt their lonely hardships through a deepening winter's freeze,
Have seen the steadfast women press their face against the pane,
Waiting for their sons' return in driving sleet and rain.
Seen them after winter's thaw as they walk the garden way,
Setting out their plotted land at the break of early day.
The land hadn't much to offer, with its hills denude of soil,
For the only thing it offered was a life of sweat and toil.
Can this be what they came for, risking life and soul,
Who settled in those inlets, the family name of Noel?

When they came and why they came, is through the ages lost
Still I seek the answer with each grassy meadow's frost.
What was it like those days of old to sight the virgin lands,

To cut and build a homestead with axe and calloused hands?
It took them years to clear the land and get the seeds to grow,
For the elements knew no mercy with its cold wind, rain and snow.
Still they built themselves a monument, a testament of their toil,
They left for us the stony walls, a cleared and rocky soil.
When they came and why they came, we seek the answer more,
For the date we know it not, when they sailed unto this shore.

I have felt the summer breezes, like God's hand upon my brow,
And found a peace within me as my head I gently bow.
When I journeyed up the hillside, as ancestors did of old,
To watch an evening sunset, with its many stories told.
Marvelled at the masterpiece which God alone can paint,
Seeking out the answer, was it plan or was it fate,
That led them from their homeland, across an unknown sea,
To start their life anew, where mortal souls were free?
I lay there in the darkness, scanning the mysteries of the sky,
Still! there seemed to be no answers, for what? and when? and why?

This poem is dedicated to my grandparents George A. Noel and Gertrude Parsons Noel, and to those early Noels who settled in the bays and inlets of Newfoundland known by the names of Clement, Mary, Jonathan, John, William, James, George, Peter, Thomas, Jane, Philip, Mark, etc. Also to Norman C. Krischke of Schulenburg, Texas, who took this tiny thread between the past and present, which was almost lost in obscurity, and with it linked the roots and branches of the Noel Family Tree. Our grandfather, George A. Noel (1888-1971), said the Noels were French Huguenots from Alsace-Lorraine. They left France the day of, or the day after, the Saint Bartholomew's Day Massacre, (August 24-25,1572), and went to the Channel Islands between England and France. Sometime in the mid-1700s they migrated to Freshwater, Conception Bay North, Newfoundland. The first Noel to arrive was Clemence (Clement) Noel.

Clement Noel - Born 1715
Jersey Islands UK
Had a Son
John Noel
Had a Son
Jonathan Moores Noel
Had a Son
John Noel
Had a Son
William Noel
My Great Grandfather

Huguenot Cross

John and Susannah (Fraize) Noel
Son of Jonathan Moores Noel
Great Great Grandson of Clement

Cemence (Clement) Noel, the first Noel in Freshwater, had two sons, John and Clement. John remained there and Clement Jr. moved to Harbour Grace.

I Dreamed In A Dream

I dreamed in a dream I was home last night
Where waters kiss the dawn's first light,

I have felt the summer breezes, like God's hand upon my brow,
And found a peace within me as my head I gently bow.

I Was Home Last Night

*I saw rolling hills so tall and clear
Being washed by mist of morning air.*

*When I journeyed up the hillside, as ancestors did of old,
To watch an evening sunset, with its many stories told.*

When evening tides are rising in a glowing sunset burn,
I will toward your coastline, my weary footsteps turn.

Noels' Bus Service

Photo courtesy of Joseph G. Noel   *Colour by Dennis Flanders*

Historical Freshwater
Conception Bay North
Newfoundland and Labrador, Canada

Freshwater is one of Canada's oldest settlements with a history dating back to the 1600s. It began as a small fishing community on the rockbound coast of Newfoundland, located along the craggy shoreline of Conception Bay North in two shallow coves -- *Freshwater* and *Clowns* -- where lofty headlands meet the sky.

Its first recorded residents were Joseph Parsons, his wife, and five children, at Clowns Cove, 1697

During the French British wars, Freshwater was to play a pivotal role in maintaining an English presence in Newfoundland. In 1696-1697 and 1705 the French army attacked many communities along the shores of Conception Bay, plundering and destroying the settlements in their wake. The settlers from Carbonear and the surrounding area moved to Carbonear Island.

Legend has it the French never entered the settlement of Freshwater. As a boy growing up in this quaint historic town, I recall the elder residents referring to the road that runs over Freshwater Hill as the "Battery." It was here on this strategic headland that overlooks Carbonear Island and the entrance to Carbonear Harbour that the invading army was stopped. We are told that the French were never able to advance into Freshwater as the soldiers and fisherfolk of the town who manned the garrison fought them back. The bodies of the soldiers killed in the battles were buried in Freshwater in unmarked graves near the old British garrison.

I remember the old cannons on Freshwater Hill. One was located along the coastline between Clowns Cove and Freshwater Cove in Butt's garden. It has since been moved and put on display at Harbour Rock Hill in Carbonear. The other was stationed on Freshwater Hill where the garrison once stood. It disappeared within the past 30 years, leaving the history of this small town to pass into obscurity. All that remains is the fading ghost of a time that was. It was a world whose citizens fought the elements, hardships, disease and the storms of war, seeking a better tomorrow. Like those of many old Newfoundland communities, the early settlers who came to Freshwater did so to escape oppression and to find freedom in a new world. What they found was a lawless society where drunkenness and disorder reigned. They lost family members to ravaging disease and fought relentless storms to harvest the fruits of the sea. With sweated brow and bent back they cleared an untamed land to feed their animals and grow crops. Through it all they prevailed to become a proud and God-fearing people who left their mark on generations to come.

The first settlers of this picturesque village are believed to have come here with the fishing admirals during the summer fishing season and never returned in autumn as required by English Law at that time. No one knows for certain. We do know that many of the early pioneers came here from the British Isles and the Channel Islands. One such settler was Clemence (Clement) Noel (an ancestor of mine) who came here from the Isle of Jersey some time in the 1700s. He was one of the earliest Methodist followers in the area. Lawrence Coughlan, the first Methodist missionary to Newfoundland, often visited him in Freshwater and after Coughlan returned to England they continued to correspond, as evidenced by a letter Clement wrote to Mr. Coughlan in 1774 where he quotes, "for it is a rough and thorny road that we are walking in; but, I know that the Lord will deliver us out of all our troubles here below."

By 1800 and into the early 1900s, Freshwater had a railroad station, courthouse, post office, telegraph office, church and a school. There were also hat and mattress factories, and several mercantile stores: Parsons, Hillyards, Butts and Moores, which helped to fill the needs of the community.

They grew vegetables, raised animals, participated in the yearly seal hunt, built houses and fishing premises, and raised families to be self-sufficient. Some went to the Labrador to fish when necessary and returned in the fall. In winter, some men worked in the lumber and mining industries or went to Canada or the United States to seek employment. They were industrious, hard working and God-fearing people. In later years, many young people left the fishing industry to become tradesmen, carpenters, plumbers and mechanics, while others went on to higher education and became teachers, doctors, clergymen, lawyers and businessmen.

As the clouds of war rolled across Europe in 1914 and again in 1939, many young people from Freshwater answered the call and marched off to war, back to the lands of their ancestors to defend the freedom they had sought and won so long ago.

In the changing winds of time you can hear the whispering roll call of the old family names of the past and present: Parsons, Moores, Davis, Pike, Butt, Penney, Whidler, Noel, Pottle, Sweet, Dolby, Cahill, Hammond and Joyce. Many of the names have long since left with the ebbing tide of life, leaving as the only reminder they were here an entry in an old church record or an inscription on a weather-beaten grave marker in the old church cemetery by the winding brook that flows onward to the sea from whence they came.

www.Freshwater-Carbonear.com

Cannon that was in Butt's Garden, Freshwater
Now on Display on Harbour Rock Hill, Carbonear

*The winding brook
flows onward to the sea
from whence they came.*

Old Cemetery on the right.

The Early Recorded Surnames Of Freshwater
1600 - 1800

DATE	NAME SECTION
1665 Parsons	Clowns Cove
1668 Moores	Freshwater
1713 Davis	Clowns Cove
1747 Pike	Clowns Cove
1747 Butt	Clowns Cove
1761 Penney	Freshwater
1766 Whidler	Freshwater
1766 Pottle	Clowns Cove
1774 Noel	Freshwater
1791 Dolby	Freshwater
1791 Cahill	Freshwater
1795 Hammond	Freshwater
1799 Joyce	Freshwater
1802 Grant	Freshwater
1803 Jeffers	Freshwater
1814 Canning	Freshwater
1818 Vatcher	Freshwater
1820 Barrett	Freshwater
1823 Bemister	Freshwater
1826 Hunt	Freshwater
1828 Callahan	Freshwater
1830 Clark	Freshwater
1831 Harvey	Clowns Cove
1832 Brodericks	Freshwater
1849 Corbin	Freshwater
1851 Howell	Freshwater
1855 Hiscock	Freshwater
1855 Hillyard	Freshwater
1855 Harris	Freshwater
1871 Good	Freshwater

This list was compiled from the book, Family Names of the Island of Newfoundland, by E. R. Seary, the Plantation Book and other sources. These family names may have been there for many years before they were first recorded.

Places That Were
Flatrock, Blow Me Down and Otterbury

Above Freshwater, along the shoreline stretching from Clowns Cove Head to Salmon Cove Head, were three thriving communities: Flatrock, Blow Me Down and Otterbury. I say "were," for today all you can see of those former villages is a sea of wild grass waving in a lazy breeze on a summer's morn, as if saying farewell to a people passed. But, in the glow of a late autumn sunset as its shadows of evening fade into winter night, you can hear, feel and see the barren desolation of *Places That Were.*

Like Freshwater in bygone years, they were busy fishing communities populated with the same brave breed of men and women who came to these shores seeking a new life. They were a hardworking, industrious people trying to make a living under difficult conditions. Unlike Freshwater and Clowns Cove, they had no beaches on which to bring their catch ashore. Some of the fishermen of Flatrock used Clowns Cove beach, but others, including those from Blow Me Down and Otterbury, built stage heads beneath the cliffs and lowered ladders down the rocky ledges to them. Then, after their catch was split, gutted and headed, they would haul it in hand barrels up to the windswept headlands above to be cured on fish flakes (drying racks) built there.

They were truly iron men who manned wooden boats, a brave and hardy race who laboured from the cliffs against a restless tide and unforgiving elements. They survived only through brute force and fortitude with a vision of a better tomorrow for their families.

They were closely related with Freshwater and were part of the social community. They were members of the social fraternal organizations, such as the Orange Lodge and the Fisherman's Union, and shared common public facilities (post office, courthouse, school and church) located in Freshwater. Many were members of the Freshwater Methodist Church. In the early days the people of those communities attended church and school in Freshwater, but later, in the first half of the 1900s, they came to have their own school and church. However, these still came under the charge of the Freshwater Methodist Church.

As the people from those communities passed away, they were buried in the cemeteries in Freshwater, so today one can see grave markers bearing inscriptions of the old familiar surnames that first settled there: Pottle, Penney, Hiscock, Evely, Derring, Clark, Snow, Wareham, Sommers, and others.

As a child I attended Church Bible school in Flatrock during the summer. But, what I remember most is going there with my friends during the winter. There were no electric lights. I was entranced by the glow of the kerosene oil lamps and the brightly burning embers from the coal and wood stoves shining through the windows and reflecting on the snow-covered ground. I can still smell the fragrance of the burning wood, coal, and the sweet aroma of the alders as it filled the frosty air.

By the time I was a youth, there were only a few families living in Blow Me Down and Otterbury. The fishing industry diminished and the people moved out into bigger centers. Flatrock lasted until the 1960s and then, like so many small communities throughout Newfoundland, they too went the path of resettlement. But the descendants of this small community still maintain a linkage to their heritage by celebrating Flatrock Day once a year. It's a day when elders remember and the young folk hear the stories retold of – A Time That Was – Places That Were. But to their ancestors, it was – *A Place Called Home.*

Flatrock

A Map of Freshwater Conception Bay North

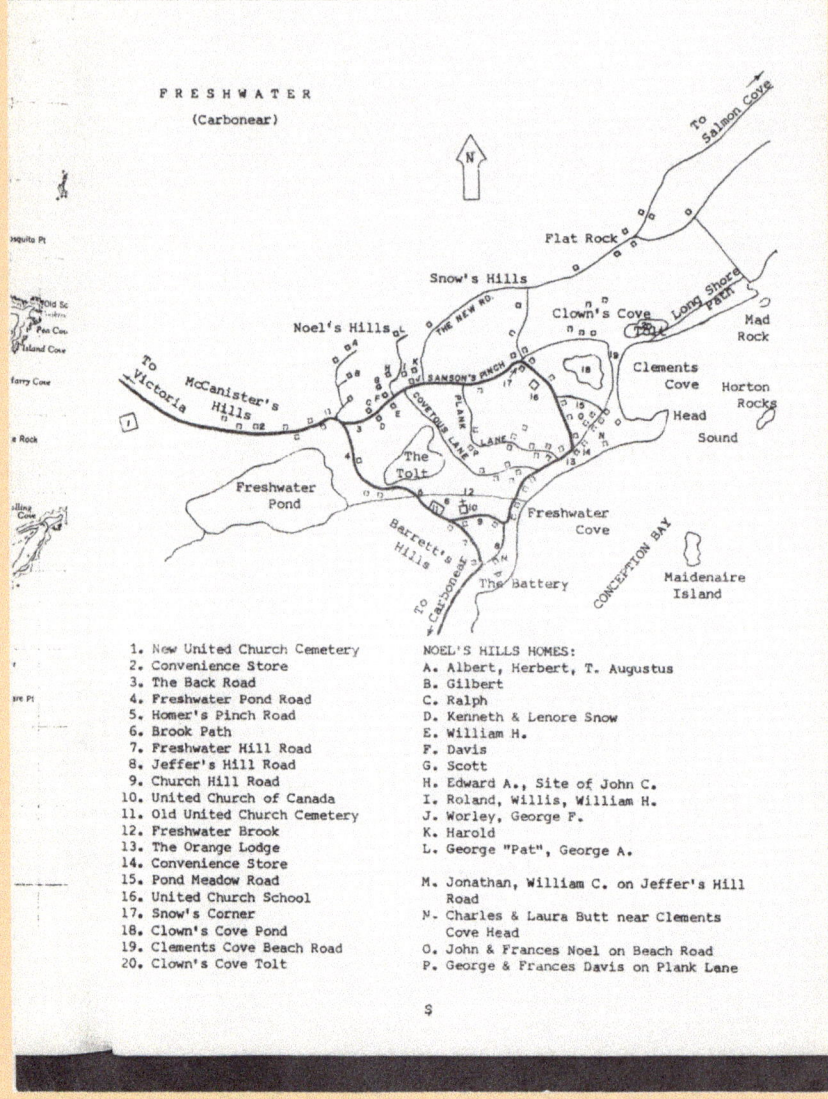

This is the map of Freshwater that I drew for Norman C. Krischke for inclusion in his book, Gathering Up All the Noels (1981).

Plantation Book
1806

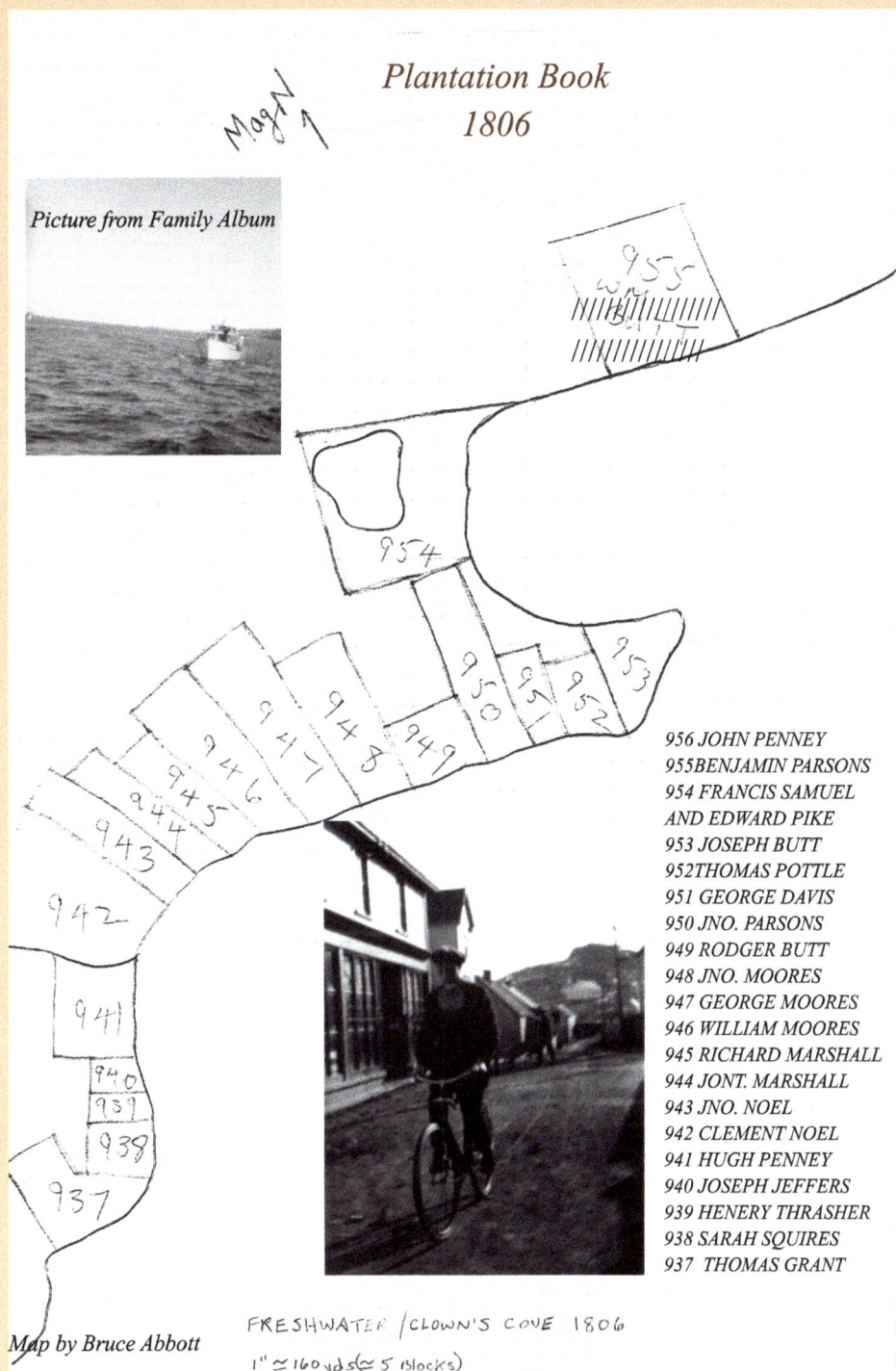

Picture from Family Album

956 JOHN PENNEY
955 BENJAMIN PARSONS
954 FRANCIS SAMUEL AND EDWARD PIKE
953 JOSEPH BUTT
952 THOMAS POTTLE
951 GEORGE DAVIS
950 JNO. PARSONS
949 RODGER BUTT
948 JNO. MOORES
947 GEORGE MOORES
946 WILLIAM MOORES
945 RICHARD MARSHALL
944 JONT. MARSHALL
943 JNO. NOEL
942 CLEMENT NOEL
941 HUGH PENNEY
940 JOSEPH JEFFERS
939 HENERY THRASHER
938 SARAH SQUIRES
937 THOMAS GRANT

Map by Bruce Abbott

FRESHWATER / CLOWN'S COVE 1806
1" ≃ 160 yds (≃ 5 blocks)

Picture from Family Album

134								
950	Jno. Parsons 53 yds from E to W bounded on the E by Geo Davis on the W by Rodger Butt 208 yds from HWM to the NW bounded on the NW by the woods 1 Stage 4 Flakes 4 Houses 3 Gardens 2 Meadows	Clowns Cove	Clowns Cove	By deed of gift from his Father	Jno Parsons	Not sold or leased	1755	
134								
951	George Davis 36 yds from E to W bounded on the E by Thos. Pottle on the W by John Parsons 95 yds from HWM to the N bounded on the N by Jno Parsons 1 House 3 Gardens	Clowns Cove	Clowns Cove	By deed of gift from his Father	Geo. Davis	Not sold or leased	1803	
134								
952	Thomas Pottle 61 yds from E to W bounded on the E by Joseph Butt on the W by Geo. Davis 70 yds from HWM to the N bounded on the N by the Path 1 House 1 Garden	Clowns Cove	Clowns Cove	Purchased from Thos. Whidler for £8	Ths. Pottle	Not sold or leased	1766	
134								
953	Joseph Butt 80 yds from E to W bounded on the E by the Sea on the W by Thos. Pottle 108 yds from S to N bounded on the S and N by the Sea 1 Stage 1 Flake 2 Houses 1 Garden	Clowns Cove	Clowns Cove	Purchased from John Pike for £20.	Jos. Butt	Not sold or leased	1747	
134								
954	Francis Samuel and Edward Pike 137 yds from S to N by the Seaside bounded on the S by John Parsons on the N by a mountain 146 yds to the W bounded on the W by the woods. 1 Stage 2 Flakes 1 Beach 2 Houses 4 Gardens 2 Meadows	Clowns Cove	Clowns Cove	By deed of gift from their Father	F.S. & Edw. Pike	Not sold or leased	1800	
135								
955	Benjamin Parsons 50 yds from E to W 40 from S to N bounded on all sides by the woods 1 House 1 Garden	Clowns Cove	Clowns Cove	Cut out of woods	B. Parsons	Not sold or leased	1795	
135								
956	John Penny 80 yds from E to W 90 yds from S to N bounded on all sides by the woods 1 House 1 Garden	Clowns Cove	Clowns Cove	Cut out of woods	John Penny	Not sold or leased	1796	

Each Boy On His Nansarey
For The Down Hill Run

Pictures from the Old Family Album

John Butt; Dale, Roland and Davis Noel; Raymond Penney

Plantation Book Freshwater - Carbonear

1805

Page and Lot No.	Name and Description Of The Room And Other Erections with its Exact Boundaries	In what Harbour cove, ect., Situated	Name and Residence of the Party Claiming Right to the Same	The Nature of the Claim	Name and Residence of the present Occupier	Whether Built, Sold or Leased at the time of this Entry	Date of this Entry	To Whom So Leased or otherwise Transferred
133 937	Thomas Grant 68yds.from E to W bounded on the E by Sarah Squires on the W by John Harvey and Robt. Joyce 120 yds from HWM to the N bounded on the N by the Commons 1 Stage 3 Flakes 2 Houses 2 Gardens 1 Meadow	Freshwater	Freshwater	Purchased from Rd Dolby for £80	Thomas Grant	Not sold or leased	1802	
133 938	Sarah Squires 70 yds from E to W bounded on the E by Henry Thrasher on the W by Thomas Grant 70 yds from HWM to the N bounded on the N by the Path 1 House 1 Garden	Freshwater	Freshwater	Purchased from Richd. Dolby and Jno Sweet for £55	Ed. Cahill F Water	Not sold or leased	1791	Leased to Ed for 11 years 1 £2.15
133 939	Henry Thrasher 70 yds E. to W. bounded on the E by Joe Jeffers on the W by the Commons 36 yds from HWM to the N bounded on the N by the Commons 1 Flake 2 Houses 1 Garden	Freshwater	Freshwater	Purchased from Thos. Hammond for £24	No person	Not sold or leased	1795	
133 940	Joseph Jeffers 70 yds from HWM to the Westward bounded on the W by Henry Thrasher 30 yds from S to N bounded on the S by Henry Thrasher on the N by Hugh Penny 1 Stage 2 Flakes 1 House 1 Garden	Freshwater	Freshwater	Do from G & Jas Kemp & Co for £40	Jos. Jeffers	Not sold or leased	1803	
133 941	Hugh Penny 110 from HWM to the W bounded on the W by the Commons 91 yds from S to N bounded on the S by Joseph Jeffers on the N by the Brook 1 Stage 3 Flakes 4 Houses 1 Garden 1 Meadow	Freshwater	Freshwater	Purchased from Jno. Cadwell for £10	H. Penny	Not sold or leased	1781	
133 942	Clement Noel 73 yds from E to W bounded on the E by John Noel on the W by the Brook 200 yds from HWM to the N bounded N by the woods 1 Stage 2 Flakes 3 Houses 3 Gardens 1 Meadow	Freshwater	Freshwater	Bequeathed to him by his father's will	Ct. Noel	Not sold or leased	1795	
133 943	Jno. Noel 51 yds from E to W bounded on the E by Jona Marshall on the W by Clement Noel 198 yds from HWM to the N bounded on the N by a mountain 1 Stage 1 Flake 4 Houses 2 Gardens 1 Meadow	Freshwater	Freshwater	By deed of gift from his Father	Jno Noel	Not sold or leased	1777	
134 944	Jont. Marshall 30 yds from E to W bounded on the E by Richd. Marshall on the W by Jno. Noel 191 yds from HWM to the N bounded on the N by the woods 1 Stage 1 Flake 1 House 1 Garden 1 Meadow	Freshwater	Jont. Marshall F.W.	Bequeathed to him by his Father's will	Jont. Marshall	Not sold or leased	1803	
134 945	Richard Marshall 46 yds from E to W bounded on the E by Wm Moores on the W by Jonathan Marshall 184 yds from HWM to the N bounded on the N by the woods 1 Flake 1 House 1 Garden 1 Meadow	Freshwater	Jont. Marshall F.W.	By deed of gift from his Grandfather	R. Marshall	Not sold or leased	1792	
134 946	William Moores 60 yds from E to W bounded on the E by Geo. Moores on the W by R Marshall 191 yds from HWM to the N bounded on the N by the woods 1 Stage 1 Flake 2 Houses 1 Garden 1 Meadow	Freshwater	W Moores	By deed of gift from his Grandfather	W.M.	Not sold or leased	1781	
134 947	George Moores 58 yds from E to W bounded on the E by Jno. Moores on the W by Wm Moores 196 yds from HWM to the N bounded on the N by the woods 1 Stage 1 Flake 2 Houses 1 Garden 1 Meadow	Freshwater	W Moores	By deed of gift from his Grandfather	G.M.	Not sold or leased	1780	
134 948	Jno. Moores 53 yds from E to W bounded on the E by Roger Butt on the W by Wm Moores 181 yds from HWM to the N bounded on the N by the woods 1 Stage 1 Flake 2 Houses 2 Gardens	Freshwater	W Moores	By deed of gift from his Grandfather	Jno. Moores	Not sold or leased	1773	
134 949	Rodger Butt 86 yds from E to W bounded on the E by Jno. Parsons on the W by Jno Moores 71 yds from HWM to the N bounded on the N by the Path 1 Stage 1 Flake 2 Houses 2 Gardens	Freshwater	W Moores	Purchased from Jno. Moores for £8	R Butt	Not sold or leased	1770	

I found this information when searching the Plantation Book at the Registry of Deeds in St. John's in 1998. There were families in Freshwater and Clowns Cove many years before their lands were registered.

www.Freshwater-Carbonear.com

Clowns Cove, Freshwater

*John Harvey Butt's Homestead
Where I was Born in 1941 into a World Gone Insane*

Photos from my grandfather Charles Butt's photo album

I Dreamed in A Dream
September 27, 1963

I dreamed in a dream I was home last night
Where waters kiss the dawn's first light,
I saw rolling hills so tall and clear
Being washed by mist of morning air.

I saw the house where I was born,
One frosty, stormy winter morn,
And the little town and where it lay
Nestled in a cove in Conception Bay.

I saw the village with its houses white
In gleam and dance of a northern light,
The school house where we would meet
On that ribbon of clay we called a street.

And there appeared before my eyes,
A colorful cluster of girls and boys,
Running, playing with smiles so grand,
The pride and joy of any land.

In the distance, I heard a roar
Waves pounding on a rock bound shore
And an old foghorn's mournful sound
Warning mariners of rocks abound.

It was here I woke to a predawn light
From a dream, in a dream, I dreamt last night.

Pulling Cod Trap Near Easter Rock
Andrew Parsons and Crew

The men of Freshwater, from its first settlers in the 1600s, were men of the sea. They fished the Newfoundland shore and Labrador waters. Others were part of the crew on ships that sailed the seven seas.

Photo Courtesy of Clayton Parsons

L-R Herder Noel, Herbert Parsons, Albert Noel and Andrew Parsons

The Twillingate Sun
October 6, 1882

The schooner Happy Home, of Fresh Water, Conception Bay put in here for medical aid last evening, having on board Richard Moores of Carbonear, who was shot in the forearm by the accidental discharge of a shot gun on Monday last at Dead Island, Labrador inflicting an extensive wound, carrying away all the principal muscles from the under and outer side of the left forearm between the wrist and elbow, exposing the ulnar, and slightly fracturing the radial bones. Considering the extent of the wound the the patient was doing moderately well and as the wind was favorable, Dr. Scott after rendering such assistance as was immediately necessary, and after consulting the Port Commissioner, Josiah Colbourne Esq., J.P., who also rendered such assistance as lay in his power, advised that the schooner should proceed at once to her destination, where constant medical attendance might save the arm or in the event of its progressing unfavorably, amputation would be imperative.

The schooner had on board about 200 qtls. of fish with the usual quantity of oil - and about 70 persons young and old returning from the fisheries. When we consider the discomforts so strikingly manifested on board of vessels going and returning from the fisheries, from overcrowding and in the event of accidents or sickness, the suffering and loss of life which may at any time accrue, it appears strange that the salutary saturating enactment passed last session is not more rigorously enforced.

The Twillingate Sun
September 22, 1882

Heroism Rewarded We have great pleasure in noting a fresh instance of the humane and courageous conduct, for which Newfoundland seamen are proverbial, which has received fitting recognition.

The schooner Kestrel, Capt. Joyce belonging to Messrs. John Munn & Co., Harbor Grace, when on a voyage from Labrador to Naples in October last, fell in with the wreck of the brigantine Busy Bee, of Nova Scotia. There was a very high sea at the time and the boarding of the wreck was a work fraught with difficultly and imminent peril. But Capt. Joyce and his crew were equal to the occasion and three gallant fellows promptly volunteered to dare all in the noble effort to save life. They succeeded in getting off four of the hands on board of the Busy Bee. When night closed in it was decided to allow the remainder of the crew to remain on board till morning and to lie by the wreck meanwhile.

At daylight the same men went off again to finish their good work and experienced quite as much difficulty and danger as on the night before. The sea was still equally rough. Complete success, however, now crowned their labors as they brought on board the Kestrel the five men and one woman who had been on board the Busy Bee during the night.

It is gratifying to know that their heroic act has been acknowledged by the Government of Canada with the present of a silver watch to each of the men engaged in the rescue, viz - To Capt. JOYCE, Joseph BRAZIL, Thomas BEMISTER and John BUTT. His Honor the Administrator has received the watches for presentation. – *Newfoundlander.*

Transcribed from the original documents, including spelling differences.

Rescue Of Brigantine Busy Bee
By
The Schooner Kestrel

To John H. Butt for his gallant human exertion in rescueing the ship-wreck crew Busy Bee.

Photo courtesy of Charlie Butt, great grandson of John Harvey Butt

Rescue took place October.21,1881

Sailor John H. Butt
Photo courtesy great-granddaughter Gee Noel Dwyer

I dedicate this poem to my great-grandfather, John H. Butt (Sailor Johnny) of Freshwater, who sailed many seas and was one of three sailors from the schooner Kestrel who in a raging storm volunteered to go in a lifeboat and rescue the crew and passengers of the brigantine Busy Bee.

Capt Joyce of Carbonear, John H. Butt, Thomas Bemister of Freshwater and Joseph Brazil of Harbour Grace, were awarded silver watches from the Government of Canada for their gallant bravery.

It's Nights Like This
1962

It's nights like this old sailors walk
On an ocean carpet green,
In dim of light, they tell their tales
Of nightmare days they've seen.

Talk of nights, when winds blew free
When the seas were a boiling roar,
How they sailed ships in a perilous sea,
Sought shelter along a wave-lashed shore.

They tell their tale of a serpent moon
Making the billowing waters sweep,
With skies alight, like the flames of hell
Where they saw souls of men run deep.

It is here old Neptune rides the tide
Lending the devil a meddling hand,
Plotting sailors their final course,
To their heavenly promised land.

It's nights like this old women talk
How they walked a creaking floor,
Waited in silence for their sons' return
And walk through an open door.

Yes! It is nights like this old sailors talk
Of the dark and the deep blue sea,
Drink a toast to the good old days,
How they brought tattered ships alee.*

Lee- the side of something that is sheltered from the wind

Sunset Over Freshwater Pond

The Long Wait
May 11, 1958

On a sea beaten shore stood a little girl one day,
Waiting for her father who was, oh, so far way,
She scarcely knew her father for he was on the roam
Sailing his ocean liner upon the surging foam.
Her mother had told her, "Go watch the ocean line,"
For her father was returning from across the salty brine.
Week after week she waited, but her father did not come
Yet, still there she waited where surging waters run.
Then one morning as she watched the ocean line
In the long narrow harbour, ships she numbered nine
Soon she saw in that number her father's ship was not,
Then in a mournful whisper, "Oh, where can he be got?"
Yet, still on that seashore she waited many a day
Often in a church pew, you would hear her softly pray,
Asking the Lord above to return her father safely home,
"Let the North Star shine, where ere he may roam."
Then one autumn morning his ship returned at last
But in the distance didn't see the flag as it flew half-mast,
She ran into the house when she saw those sail so white,
Soon in every saddened heart there grew a glowing light

But when they saw the patron* colours red, white and blue
They knew in their hearts one was missing from the crew.
"Who was this missing seaman?" Word soon whispered round,
Within a few short moments, a veil fell o'er the town.
And as this ocean liner was escorted in and docked,
People around in countless numbers flocked.
The second-in-command came and stood upon the plank,
He had a duty to perform, he was now first in rank.
The little girl came running as her blue eyes began to tear,
"Tell me mister, mister sir, why this suit of black you wear?"
The man in black stood silent, with face distressed and white,
"The Lord took your father, one dark and stormy night.
He was standing on the bridge as raging waves ran high,
Like captains of old time, your father did bravely die.
You see, he was a hero, a mariner brave and true,
Over calm or stormy waters, he always brought us through.
But the death of your father will now record in fame,
He saved the souls of many that night on the Spanish Main
Our ship was ravaged by wind and storm, as any ship could be,
We owe our lives to your father who brought us o'er the sea.
And now little girl, wipe those weeping eyes so blue
I know that on the Golden Shore your father waits for you."
She still was crying when walking sadly home that day
When in a lonely bugle note, she heard her father say,
"Loving, little daughter, you waited many days for me,
And now I'll longingly wait for you, on heaven's eternal sea."

* ***The Meaning of the Union Jack:*** *The vertical and horizontal red lines form the cross of Saint George, patron saint of England. The diagonal red lines form the cross of St. Patrick, patron saint of Ireland. The diagonal white cross is Saint Andrew's, patron saint of Scotland.*

Photos by Justin Noel

A Walk Through Freshwater

View From Noel's Hill

Freshwater Pond From The Tolt - Barrett's Hills (left)

Looking Out The Bay

McCannister's And Noel's Hills (right)

Panorama created by Dennis Flanders

Sunrise Over Conception Bay North

She stands there like a diamond in the shadow of the Tolt
The music from her choir hits every sinner's note.

Photo by Gee Noel Dwyer

Freshwater United Church

Her spire was a beacon to old sailors of the sea,
They used it as a landmark from port side to their lee.

Photo by Glenys Noel Flanders

We are not quite sure when the first church was built in Freshwater. However, we do know in 1838 the foundation was complete. In 1839, its cornerstone was laid, but 1842 records show that the church was still not finished. It was after 1842 and maybe as late as 1858, during the time of Rev. Christopher Lockhart. It is believed it was located on the waterside near Clown's Cove.   *(Rev. George Boyd, 1881)*

1881- There are records in the Provincial Wesleyan on March 4, 1881 that quote Rev. George Boyd, "I am very busy now building two new churches – one 65' by 80' the other 35' by 20' the larger one at Freshwater is in place of the old one which Bros. Lockhart had to do when on the circuit. It occupies a fine situation and is ornamented with a spire which is seen well out the bay."   *(Records in the Provincial Wesleyan on March 4, 1881)*

1883 - Freshwater became a separate Circuit under the leadership of Rev. James B. Heal, who became superintendent.
                                    Excerpt from the Freshwater United Church 80th Anniversary Booklet

1926 - A new church was erected and in 1976 the congregation celebrated its 50th anniversary and in 2006, the 80th anniversary.

In the early days of the church, the congregation was renowned for their singing and old-time preaching. It was here on Sunday mornings you would hear the church bells ringing and see families walking to church. The church has played a pivotal role in the community down through the centuries.

It was on the occasion of the 80th anniversary I wrote the poem "In The Shadow of the Tolt".

In The Shadow Of The Tolt
June 5, 2006

She stands there like a diamond in the shadow of the Tolt*
The music from her choir hits every sinner's note.
Her spire was a beacon to old sailors of the sea,
They used it as a landmark from port side to their lee.
Her foundation is built beyond the reach of man
Along with rocks and mortar was set the Master's plan.
But it is clearly written in the good books old and new
That you do unto others as you would wish them do onto you.

Then there are the voices captured within those hallowed walls.
Can you hear the old time preachers, setting up their altar calls
As they billow out their sermons, "The damnations of this world"
With a hell and brimstone message to their congregation furled?
Listen to the whispers as the faithful rise in harmony of song,
As the sinner, he steps forward to repent his right from wrong.
They are singing "Rock of Ages" and music from their past.
The *Hallelujah Chorus* – Lord, I am coming home at last.

Many years have rolled beyond her and she saw her world at war,
Watched her sons and daughters leave home to return no more.
She has always been a refuge through anguish, death and strife
Still she is giving comfort with the hope of eternal life.
While her belfry is still calling as her bell tolls to and fro
Her window panes still sparkle when the harvest moon is low.
Its sanctuary – a holy place, where reverently you tread
For it holds the cherished memories of the living and the dead.

Her structure is still standing and has stood the test of time
A testament to the architects and the builders of this shrine
For she is a shining temple – a living mansion on the hill
Eighty years going forward and still doing the Master's will
She is like the subservient Shepherd caring for her flock
In Freshwater, Clown's Cove, Otterbury, Blow me Down and Flatrock.

---

* *A Tolt is a high hill overlooking the ocean. In the early days of settlement in Newfoundland, it was used as a lookout for pirate and enemy war ships. Tolt is an old English word meaning high hill.*

They Set Out Their Plotted Land

At The Break of Early Day

No Matter Where You Journey

You Will Find No Place Like Home:

Home Is Where The Heart Resides

She Saw Not Life
April 6, 1959

She was a child, four months no more,
She did not hear the billows roar
Nor see the sun set on the bay,
For Lord you called her far away.
Why did you claim her for your own?
Why you so early called her home?
From her unknown family dear,
Whose short life, they all did share.

She did not know this world of strife,
For in this world she saw not life,
She did not see the flowering earth
Or know the price that life is worth
For her I know you must have need,
To take from earth this little seed.

To my sister Beverley who died at the age of four months.

Photo courtesy of Audrey Maciel

Spring in Freshwater
1979

Maiden Island, Carbonear Island, Harbour Grace Island

N.B. The locals call it Maidenear Island but the correct name is Maiden Island

Photo by Justin Noel

Tucker Mills

Rock located in Freshwater is named for two men from Carbonear: Tucker and Mills. A sudden storm came up late one night when they were returning to Carbonear after visiting friends in Freshwater or Clowns Cove. Their boat struck this rock and they drowned.

Another version of the story is they were bird hunting from this rock and fell off and drowned.

Pictures from the Old Family Album

Thomas Butt   Al Broderick   Laura Butt   Charles Butt

Orange Young Britain Meeting

Getting Ready for The Garden Party

Girls Taking A Rest In Clowns Cove

Girls Gather in W. J. Moores' Store Doorway.

At The Garden Party

1st row L-R Laura (Ollie) Butt, Mabel Noel, Roland Noel, Nellie Snow, Mrs. Butler, Janie Butt.
2rd row L-R Mary Butt, Lizzie Parsons, Dot Parsons, Susie Penny, Cecily Howell, Sophie Davis.
3rd row L-R Mary Howell, Susie Butt, Mary Clarke, Mary Davis, Emmeline Butt, Marion Davis

Looking Out The Bay

Freshwater Hill

I think not of wars fought around the whole world wide,
But only of the unsung men who in this battle died,

Growing up in this small community we were told that during the French - English War (1696-1697, 1705) the French never entered Freshwater, and the story of the ghost of a drummer boy who in mid-winter ran through town warning villagers of the approaching French army.

Another story told by my great-uncle, Thomas Butt, was of a Mr. Davis who lived across the gardens from them. Early one summer morning he looked through his bedroom window and saw two French soldiers in full military dress cutting the grass in his backyard. He turned to call his wife to look, but when he turned back the soldiers were gone. As the story goes, the grass never grew on that spot of land again.

I wrote the following poem after reading an article titled, "History Should Be Marked" in the Newfoundland Quarterly, 1959. It was signed, "a Freshwater Archivist".

Freshwater Stood Unconquered
May 5, 1958

I stood there on the hillside that overlooks the bay
And there for just awhile my mind it went astray
I thought of wars fought long ago around the whole world wide,
Of men who with valiant hearts in bloody battles died
And generals planning battles like some unholy game,
On monuments around the world, inscribed you'll find their name.

Then my mind it wandered back to my native Newfoundland:
French and English wars were fought on soil where now I stand.
D'Iberville, the French General, a soldier of some reknown,
On invading Conception Bay, he crushed town after town.
St. John's, Harbour Grace and Carbonear were no easy task
Yet, in the town of Freshwater, settlers there stood fast.

Some settlers did evacuate to the Island of Carbonear,
For this French General, the settlers did greatly fear.
But the Island of Carbonear the French could ne'er invade,
As on Freshwater Hill the balance of power weighed,
How the battle it went forth has been lost with passing time,
To the English on that day, this hill was a hallowed shrine.

After many an hour battle, the French had to retreat.
As on Freshwater Hill, D'Iberville his match did meet,
Now in Freshwater two nations lie side by side,
No monuments stand to show where they fought and died,
Nor crosses mark their plots where now in peace they lie,
On this lone strategic hill, no nations' flags do fly.

Now, when visiting that hillside looking o'er the bay,
Standing there -- no longer do my thoughts drift astray --
I think not of wars fought around the whole world wide,
But only of the unsung men who in this battle died,
Fisherfolks who fought with musket, pick and spade,
Protecting their New - Found - Land, down their lives they laid.

View from Freshwater Hill

Freshwater Cove

View From Freshwater Hill, Maiden Island

Carbonear Island

View From Freshwater Hill

Towards Crockers Cove

Clowns Cove

Fishing stages at the base of Long Shore Path which ran along the side of the cliff that runs between Clowns Cove and Flatrock.

Pictures from the Old Family Album

Freshwater Men Home from Hunting

Freshwater Cove

Young Men Dressed in Their Sunday Best

The Packet Boat Saint Patrick

During the first week of December 1840, the Packet Boat Saint Patrick ran aground on the rocks off Clowns Cove Head during a raging snowstorm. There were ten people aboard at the time, made up of crew and passengers. Six people were rescued and four people died.

Down through the years some people in Clowns Cove and Freshwater say they have heard the baffling of the sails and voices of the people on the ship crying out for help. The local people call it "the hollows on the sound." It was from this story I got the inspiration to wrote the poem The Lovely Antoinette.

The Shoal Rocks of Clowns Cove Head, Freshwater, Conception Bay, Newfoundland. I took this picture 172 years after the ship went down.

The Lovely Antoinette
December 5, 1957

It is on this lonely rough and rugged shore
Where often times bitter winds do rage and roar.
Often here I sit and think of the lovely Antoinette,
When trying to save her father, met a premature death.

She was a fisherman's daughter, who fished from out the land
Living in a rockbound cove on the shores of Newfoundland,
She adored her doting father and dearly loved him true
And many a time with him she sailed along as crew.

One day a wind blew strong, when changing from the south.
And in every cove and harbour fishermen hurried about
Trying to save sheds and boats, along with fishing gear
For these northeast winds, fishermen do greatly fear.

Ten boats left their moorings this calm, cold autumn day,
In their return course those winds would fiercely lay,
For the lives of these fishermen, people did truly fear
Soon on loved ones' cheeks, teardrops would appear.

Down along the waterfront people did widely stare
All they could ever see was a watery grave out there.
They looked and stared, but nothing could they find
As o'er a wild and jagged coast flew the salty brine.

All day those anxious people most reverently did pray,
Men, both young and old, were in the storm this day.
Through wind, sea and rain was heard the ocean's roar
In many a waiting home loved ones walked the floor.

An old salt in his garden pressed a glass against his eye.
Out on a far horizon some boats he did vaguely spy
Joyful he went shouting, news throughout the town
"The boys, the boys, I saw them! They're homeward bound."

Down the path came Antoinette, racing from her home,
For her father he was out there riding that yeasty foam.
Standing on the headland with her looking glass in hand,
She watched the weary mariners heading for the land.

As she looked, her heart grew cold with fear,
Is it any wonder at what she saw out there?

Boats she was counting were numbering only nine.
Who was this lone mariner, missing from the line?

When those small, sturdy craft sailed closer to the land,
People were asking, "Who could be the missing man?"
Was it Antoinette's father, a man she loved so true
Who was the missing mariner left on the boiling blue?

Antoinette not stopping, not even to count the odds,
Ran down the windswept bank that was disrobed of sods,
She ran across the headland along the wave lashed shore,
O'er her frail, slender body did the pounding waters pour,

With all voices shouting, shouting with all their might,
"Come back, Antoinette! He'll be home by fall of night."
Yet she refused to listen and ignored their pleading call,
Her mind was only out where waves did rise and fall.

Then much to their surprise, they saw her in the boat
Through wind, rain and storm, saw her heading out.
Down along the coast she went tossing on the foam,
Her father, he was out there, and she'd gone to bring him home.

As the evening shadows ended, clouds of night flew by,
A beacon, from the lighthouse, pierced the stormy sky.
In every alongshore window lanterns did brightly burn
People all were praying for Antoinette's safe return.

As night was lighting to the dawn of a newborn day,
A search for Antoinette was quickly on its way.
They searched craggy coves and along the hidden shoal
It's here they found her body where heaving waters roll.

Now when autumn winds are blowing, blowing at their height,
Out on a cresting wave, an apparition comes to sight.
One of Antoinette, shining through lighted misty foam,
Her father was out there and she went to bring him home.

An Old Man's Tale
January 7, 1959

Have you ever fought your way through a blizzard of snow
Where you were wandering, you did not know?
Have you ever sat on a river snowdrift bank?
Watching your horse as through the ice it sank,
Down in the pond with its ice fault ways --
Yet, all you could do was to stare and gaze?
Ever been frostbitten, as snow cut through the bone,
When all you could hear was the fierce wind's moan?

As I went to the store on a cold winter's day,
An old, old man happened to pass my way.
He led me over and sat me down,
On his half-bearded face, he wore a frown,
As he walked along on the sawdust floor,
I saw on his face the scars he wore.
As he shuffled along on his weakened knee
He said, "Young fellow now listen to me."

"You see it was March 31, in nineteen o' four,
When a storm, from the nor 'east struck our shore,
Not looking a storm was coming our way,
So most of us headed for the woods that day,
We traveled for miles o'er the barren waste
Not knowing the hardships we were to face,
We cut and cut and we soon had our load,
So late in the evening we sought for the road."

"We looked to the west and the sky it was clear,
When we looked northeast - we saw it there.
However, we thought it was mist from the bay,
So we yelled at our horses and started our way,
Some sang, some swore, others grumbled low,
When our horses strained they began to blow.

So we gave them a rest at just about five,
As the wind had an edge like a new stoned sive."*

By the time we got started, the storm it had come
No one knew the direction we started from,
When setting our bearings to face the storm
Men jumped and ran to keep themselves warm.
Then we heard a cry from back in the line
"He's dying, he's dying" a young boy was crying,
I went back through the line to see what was wrong
There sadly discovered his father died in the storm.

As the night came on, we started to pray
For the storm to cease and to see the day,
As morning came with its snow piled high.
Even the bravest of men began to cry,
For there in the snow, were eight men stiff and white,
That died where they lay, on that cold March night.
Soon those of us left, we started for home,
To cross over lakes where wild wolves roam.

Some boys cried like a lost mother's child
As over the snow we wandered many a mile.
The road now sightless, we feared we were lost,
And men how they cursed that cold bitter frost,
When tying the strings on our parka's hood,
Our fingers felt like they were junks of wood,
And legs like frozen logs on an iced riverbank,
While our life was ebbing as the lamp flame sank.

Yet on and on we struggled our way
And sighted our road at the eve of day,
With strength all spent, we started to crawl,
When through the wind came an echoing call,

* *scythe - Locally in Newfoundland it is called a sive*

Of voices of men, who sought for our trail.
Searching for us in that God awful gale,
They led us back home to our family and friends
Telling the fate of the others, to their next of kin.
It is true - it is true - do not doubt me, young lad
When you go home just ask your Grandad.

I wrote this poem while visiting my grandparents in St. John's. I went to the grocery store where most customers were complaining about the storm. There I met an old gentleman who was explaining what winters were like in his time. I went home and wrote this poem based on his conversation.

Let Not The Winds Blow, Lord
1968

She knelt in the churchyard,
With heart heavy and cold,
Eyes that were bloodshot,
In them a story untold.

A story of a mother's love
A boy who went to sea
To face towering waves,
Fighting for our liberty.

I stood and watched her,
Heard her pray to God on high
Asking softly in a whisper,
"Let not my young son die.

Let not the storm winds blow,
Nor let the waves go mad.
Guide his ship in the night
Bring home to me my lad."

Then as I was to leave her side
Storm clouds gathered overhead
Soon the winds were blowing
Her heart grew cold with dread.

I took her by a feeble arm
Walked her to her door,
As the door I opened
The seas began to roar.

"Precious Lord," she prayed,
"Please keep his ship alee,
Let not your wild wind blow,
Calm the seas as at Galilee."

Then she told the story
The story of her life
How angry wind and wave
Caused her care and strife.

Told me of her childhood days
Of her father brave and bold
Answering the oceans whims,
Help keep family from the dole.

For her father was a seaman
Who worked the stormy wave
One day the north winds blew
He filled a mariner's grave.

"I was only a child back then,
Aged thirteen I'd say no more,
Lived out my growing years
Here on this rocky shore.

Then one day I met a man
Whom I took to be my love

He too yearned for the open sea
Just like my father up above.

About the same time of the year
When the leaves began to fall
In dying days of autumn
Old Neptune made a call.

Night before I had a dream
Like the same I had before,
Pleaded father not to go to sea,
But my plea he did ignore.

Told my love of the dream I had
A dream of sea and death
I asked him not to go to sea,
It was a wasted breath.

He did not take my heeding
Nor did he hear my call
For he yearned for open seas
And the kiss of a tempest squall.

There comes calm before a storm
That mirrors hills into the sea.
Muted skies have an eerie feel
And to God you make your plea.

Let not the winds blow, Lord
Nor let angry waves run high
Steer his ship in mist of night
Please do not let my lover die.

Yes, lost was he one stormy night
Where blustery north winds howl
Sailing through sleet and snow
In dark of night his ship ran afoul.

Last night I had another dream
Unlike the ones before
I saw my boy in a misty ray
Then never saw him more."

Slowly she looked towards me
With hair as white as snow,
"Thank you for your comfort sir
You ease my sorrow, grief and woe."

Suddenly was heard, a footstep
Then a knock upon the door
Her heart was in a drumbeat
As she shuffled across the floor.

When the door she opened
It was powdered, clouded white
That is when I came awake
In rays of an unnatural light.

Rubbed my eyes, rubbed them more
Saw my bottle of scotch was dry
Then I knew it was only a dream
When here on my bed I lie.

Somewhere Tonight Lost
November 8, 1961

Somewhere tonight there is a boy, exploring the woods unknown,
Lost is he in the wild woods that have claimed him for their own.
Cold is the dark that blinds him, damp is the mist that falls,
Somewhere out in those wild woods a lost boy frantic calls.
Calling is he for his parents, who for years have given him love,

Praying is he to his Father, who watches over him from above.
Dark is the world that he roams in, uncertain the trail he treads,
Somewhere tonight there is a brother, who sleeps alone in his bed,
Alone and sad is his brother, who walked with him on that trail,
For little they knew on that evening, as game they went to assail,
Lost would they be in the thick woods, one would be found alive,
One brought safely homeward; the other to stay there to strive.
Surviving is he in that bleak land, where bear and moose do roam,
Striving is he with the elements, that knows not the love of home,
However, kindly, kindly receiving, the things mother nature so dear,
Is putting forth in his pathway to help and to comfort his fear.
Now as the days are shortened, with its nights so wary and long,
Waiting at home is a mother, who knows not the joy of a song,
Who is hoping, longing, trusting, her boy will return in the morn.
Often there in her vision, she will see her boy stumble and fall,
Among the trees and bushes where he then begins to crawl,
His hands they are scratched, bleeding; a tear appears in his eye,
She sees him there kneeling, but awakes when she hears his cry.
Heartbroken alone is this mother, whose child is lost on the trail,
Yet, as the moments are passing -- hope for her boy does prevail,
For somewhere tonight is a father, in wild pursuit of his boy
Pushing his way through dense woods, hoping to hear his cry,
Gloomy is the world around him, inconstant the sky o'rhead,
Yet ever, ever persisting, search parties forward he led,
But, in a dawn's early morning, as the beauty of earth doth unfold,
Down by the side of a river, there is a story that will never be told.
For Mother Nature had mercy, but the elements knew nothing of love,
Therefore, God, his Heavenly Father called him to his home above.

I wrote this poem one stormy night when I heard the news of two boys that were lost in the woods in central Newfoundland.

Freshwater in a Bygone Era
Pictures from the Old Family Album

Sailor John Harvey Butt's House in Winter

Snowstorm in Freshwater
Pictures from the Old Family Album

Men Walking Along a Snowy Icy Shore Line

A Sad Christmas Day
December 23, 1958

Christmas is a time for cheers,
It is not a time for sobs and tears
It is but a time for fun and joy
What reason then for one to cry?

They were two lone people, by a fireside
Like a lone peacock, who lost one's pride.
No joy in their hearts - no gleam in their eye,
There at the table, the woman did cry.

"Why does she cry?" to me you might say.
It is because her boys are now far away,
Into the world they are now gone afar
Guided life's trail, like the shepherds the star.

This was once a home full of laughter and fun,
The boys on the carpets in bare feet would run,
Down to their stockings for candy and toys,
Waken the household with loud Christmas cries.

The years soon passed, those people are two
For into manhood those boys quickly grew.
It seems that is life. Life has its odd way,
Those people are sad on this Christmas day.

They sat at the table like lost sheep from the fold,
Outside the house blew the north wind so cold.
Silent and sadness inside, was all one could see,
When sitting in their kitchen just before tea.

As they looked through the window at eve of day,
They saw in the storm a boy plodding his way
Through snow that was blowing in wild windy air
The boy was alone and no one did care.

The man at that instant ran to the door,
Raised his voice amidst the wind's loud roar.

He then led the boy into his home,
To shelter him from the storm's angry moan.
The boy he was tired, hungry, and cold
This is the story to them he then told.

I am but a boy of fourteen, no more
Waited for years on God's wave-beaten shore,
Waiting for father to return from the sea,
He is gone to return never more to me.

They say he is home, in heaven so bright
For he was lost on a cold winter's night,
Went down in the ocean, the ocean so blue,
My brothers and sisters also went too.

My mother she died a few years ago,
She lost her way in a blizzard of snow
Leaving me without parent or home
In a world of woe to wander and roam.

Sir, would you be kind, give me a little to eat,
A place where I could rest my frostbitten feet?
This little request is all I do ask,
In my memories you forever will last.

A table was set, the food it was laid,
Over this meal God's blessing was made.
The boy did eat and was soon put to bed,
As they gave thanks, their Bibles they read.

The boy still lives with those people so gray
They will alway remember that sad Christmas day.

Christmas is a time for greetings and cheers,
To me, a time also for memories and tears,
It is a time for exchanging of gifts, they do say,
As such was the case on this sad Christmas day.

Under The Stars Of Night
November 12, 1963

Under the stars of night
Drenched with wind and rain,
Down in the woods he lay there
Crippled and racked with pain.

Cold are the winds of November,
Where you hear only rustling of trees
That seemed to softly whisper
Young man you are out here to freeze.

The wind it cuts like a whiplash,
With a sun that refuses to shine,
As misery stands in place,
Mother Nature is marking time.

Many hours had passed, since leaving the comforts of home,
To go snare a brace of rabbits, o'er the barrens he would roam,
He took with him no provisions, only his dog and gun,
Plans were to return by evening, in the glow of a setting sun.
But, soon snow and wind were blowing, as evening shadows fell,
When looking for a homeward trail, which one, he could not tell,
Soon the darkness gathered, and curtains of night were drawn,

He prayed for the quiet of morning, that proceeds a lighted dawn,
It was here in the darkness when reaching for his best friend,
An old oak tree had fallen, and had his freezing body pinned
So crippled he lay there wounded, far from friend or care,
Soon hunger, cold, and exhaustion filled his mind with fear.
He called to his dog in panic; no answer came in the dark.
For somewhere in a barnyard a lone puppy began to bark.

An old farmer hearing this lonesome howling plea,
Went running out the doorway to see what he could see.
His heart, it took a flutter, as he knelt there on one knee,
It was his grandson's puppy all covered in dirt and clay.
Suddenly he remembered, he'd gone o'er the barrens today
To catch a brace of rabbits for a future family stew,
Now he was missing, where wild winds of autumn blew.

When running down the pathway in search of a rescue crew
Overhead wild angry winds of a dying autumn blew.
Soon o'er the trail they started through sleet, wind and snow,
Led by a little puppy where studded birches grow.
Soon through the howling wind was heard an eerie ghostly cry,
Causing that faithful little puppy to go racing to and fro
Then in the flick of a lantern light flashed a body in the snow.

They moved him from his snowy grave, placed him on a sleigh,
Seeing he made no movement they most reverently did pray.
Soon, they fought their way back up the stormy trail,
Crossing faulty rivers, pushed through valley, hill and dale
While sleet and snow was blasted by driven winds on high,
But when the lighthouse beaconed, all knew they were nigh,
They headed for the old barnyard, the weary farmer's home,
They lay his lifeless body on a feathered bed like foam.

As darkness mocked the morning, dawn brought the day anew.
The sun was a misty orange bringing horizon hills in view
When mourners were gathering to say their last good-bye,
Out in a frozen field was heard a lonely puppy cry.
Then saw him run down the pathway, through an open door,
Jumping on his master, as he had done many a time before,
Yes! It was here they saw his master, come alive upon the bed,
Was this a miracle from the man who raised the dead?
Sending to all a message, saying, in this life there is no end,
Could it be that ageless bond between man and his best friend?

Man's Best Friend

Photo courtesy of Valerie Noel

Sunset And Billowing Waves
June 13, 1963

Sunset and billowing waves,
That watches o'er the wanderers' graves,
The Earth's my field, the sky my tent,
When in that field my life is spent,
Take me home to the snow clad hills
Back to rivers with their danger thrills.
To sinking of God's sun on high
A portrait he painted in the sky,
To show at the parting of life's day,
There is beauty, rest, peace: not decay
For man must die if he is born,
Bury me not in a gray early morn,

Lower me down with the sinking sun,
It is the time base; man's life must run.
Bury me as the sun dims in the west
God said, "In darkness, let man rest."
For the sun goes down to arise again,
To brighten some lone dark domain,
What the Lord giveth, he can take away
So mourn for me not on that blessed day.
For when I go down to arise again,
I will walk the road to a brighter domain.
If I should die in some adopted land
Take me back to the silver sand,
Where billowing seas do rant and roar
Seagulls scream, as on high they soar.
Oh, bury me not in the shifting sand,
But deep in the earth of my native land,
For the sands are restless they're not content
Yet that is the way my life's been spent.

The ocean in its surging cannot stay still
So place me down on a towering hill,
Keep me away from the seas' ocean might.
But in full view of the seagull's flight
For one oil slicked gull on a sea foam,
Is like a man without friend or home,
And the sea in itself is not like life untold
It never tires, weakens or ever grows old,
Wars may come, and wars may go
However, tides of the ocean will forever flow.
My life's been like a storm surging sea
So rest me high o'er where waves roll free
I know God and his mercy will understand,
He will give me rest in the depths of my land.

My one last request if I should die in my adopted land.

Sir Wilfred Grenfell
January 4, 1958

There was Sir Wilfred Grenfell on the coast of Labrador
Where many times the bitter winds do fiercely rage and roar.
He was a man of courage, which no other can compare,
When crossing the faulty ice floes, of death he had no fear.

He was the greatest of missionaries, to this he can lay claim
For all his work and courage, he won international fame.
He left his home in England, when just graduated college,
To come to the northland to practice his new found knowledge.

He left his home and comforts to come to this ice-bound land.
Where else upon this earth will you find a greater man?
Up and down the rock-bound coast, the cliffs, they saw his sails,
Many times with courage bold, he faced the raging gales.

Through dangerous icebergs his ship he would navigate,
While some stricken youngster lay waiting for his fate.
He preached the word of God when traveling on his way,
Teaching people of the north, how to serve God and to pray.

Soon the years were passing and this man was growing old,
But still undaunted he did his work in the land of snow and cold.
Then on an autumn day, this man peacefully passed away.
His great mission carries on, unto this very day.

Now in the town of St. Anthony, there a hospital bears his name,
For Grenfell gave his life and work to the land God gave to Cain.

Life's Blind Night
January 22, 1963

Say worthy lad you have traveled far,
The night grows late, 'twill be morning soon,
Why did you take this long lone road
For the night is black and there is no moon?
Oh, life's night is long, desolate, uncanny,
There are corners to turn and bridges to cross,
Time in life's night you will be alone and cold,
You will never count gains, but only your loss.

Life's blind night never seems to end,
Its wings of morning are slow to ascend,
Tho' the night be dark and the way be far,
I ask not to see each step that draws me near,
Nor in the heaven place for me a guiding star.
Through life's blind night, my light is a prayer.

Oh, Foolish Youth
March 27, 1963

Oh, foolish youth with your dreams galore
Who sails in fantasy to a far distant shore
And sees the world with a quickened glance
Comparing life's walk to a fairy dance
For man in his youth is like a cow and its pride
The grass seems greener on the other side
So he plans and plans with ambition and dream
But, oh foolish youth, with your golden sun beam
Life is like water in the mountain streams
You will follow its course as you travel along
Then find in the end it has been only a song
That rose and fell, and unheeded faded away
Foolish youth, let not your dreams lead you astray.

This I Call My Island Home
1961

This little Isle, this hollow rock, washed by the silver spray
Wars of wars she stood the shock, but still she stands today.
A cornerstone in the surging sea, whose waters cannot compare,
On ocean's crest you will see, to the world she has done her share.

Her forest green, her ponds many, and in this world of charms
You will not find more for your penny then in her bays and arms.
Her towering hills, her valleys deep, her climates number four
In a blanket of white, in winter sleeps, spreading from shore to shore.

Her running brooks, her ocean green, in springtime brings delight
Upon her bays may be seen ships sailing in the night.
Her untrod trails and unfished lakes where sportsmen love to come
In summertime to take their breaks from busy cities run.

Her scarlet slopes, sunset bright, in autumn brings mystic sight
Presents to mind an adorable view in evening's dying light.
This little fort, this strategic spot, that guards the Eastern shore
Whose waters are her seaman's plot -- their deeds: immortal lore.

This little Isle, this freedom strand, set in the inconstant foam
It is the shores of Newfoundland I call my island home.

• *Digitized Maps from the Centre for Newfoundland Studies*
Memorial University Newfoundland

In the Shadows of Even
January 21, 1962

Slowly the day was passing, curtains of night were drawn,
Wicked, lay there cursing, he would never see the morn.
Was the son of a mother who knew nothing of sin and crime,
Yet in the shadow of even', he was reminiscing time
Of the days of his childhood, a hard and wayward kid,
With a gentle mother, teaching prayers by his bed.
Girls he knew in his lifetime, schoolmates long forgot,
Came to his vision -- a loop in a hangman's knot.
Of days in drunkenness, in suffering and pain,
Days unknown and ones he would spend insane.
Money wasted and places where he dared to tread,
Mouths let go hungry as children were not fed.
Places he was taking from comrades underground,
Men falling beside him, as bombshells flew around.
"Warriors could've been doctors, builders, lawyers and such,"
Shaking his head disgusted, "To the world, I've not given much."
From darkness blind he staggered, into a lighted world
There in the shadow of even', he'd repay days absurd.
Forward went with ambition, to the world gave great gain
Now in the shadow of even, he walks down memory lane.

In my daydreams, this story came to me reliving the darker days of some unfortunate war veteran who lost his way from guilt of combat.

Port-de-Grave

Photo by © Eve Christopher Noel

The One Lost Tribe
1957

Here is a story, so sad but true,
Where waters run deep and blue,
Of people who once lived in a band:
That was genocide in Newfoundland.

In winters, they moved homes inland,
In summers, returned to sea-washed sand,
Their name was Beothuk, you see,
They roamed this Island wild and free.

Then one bright, sunny day,
Strange ships sailed into the bay,
It was here this massacre began,
Yet, Beothuk fought to the end.

As the ships approached the bay,
All the people ran away,
For the white men shot fire and lead,
In turn, they severed a white man's head.

As the years were rolling away,
More ships came sailing into the bay,
Forcing the people to the inland woods
For settlers denied them food or goods.

Now their tribe was all but gone,
In their hearts, there was no song
Due to the brutality of these men,
Their homes became a slaughter pen.

There were some near Red Indian Lake,
An Indian girl, a white man did take.
And W.E. Cormack who saw the shame,
To this fair maiden, gave acclaim.

For her name was Shanawdithit,
Intelligent, strong, and pretty
While conveying her ancestral history
Enlightened to us their tribal mystery.

There is not more that one can say
For Shanawdithit passed away
Her cause of death was tuberculosis
Among her race, it was ferocious.

She was the last of her tribe to remain,
It is said Europeans were much to blame.
No one knows of their suffering and pain,
Yet I feel their tears in a summer rain.

The Beothuk race has been long at rest
Due to men in their bloodthirst quest
And the children, how they must have cried,
This is the sad, sad story of the one lost tribe.

Photo by Gee Noel Dwyer

A statue of Shanawdithit erected in Boyd's Cove, a Beothuk site in Newfoundland. She was the last known survivor of the Beothuks or Red Indians, the aboriginals of Newfoundland. She died in St. John's June 6, 1829.

They Were Men Of Courage
February, 1957

Drake and Nelson, English sailor men of old,
Who fought for England brave and bold.
They fought the Spaniards through flame and fire,
Their deeds and bravery we still admire,
They attacked the enemy both large and small.
Fought and died to the last cannonball,
Where sailors sang as they loaded their gun,
Soon they had the Armada on the run.

Columbus sailed the ocean in fourteen ninety-two
To find new lands and commerce too,
We all know the courage of this man
He sailed weeks and weeks without sight of land,
When all his crew were as scared as could be
For he was sailing where the waves dash free
Oh, please turn back his crew did shout,
Columbus said *no*, and discovered America the South.

Now there was Sir Humphrey Gilbert the brave
Who on a royal command met his watery grave
For when taking possession of Newfoundland.
We should never forget his last command,
When out in winds where the waves dashed high
His crew cried out, *we are all going to die*,

He answered; *we are as near to heaven by sea as by land*
This was Sir Gilbert's last royal command.
There was Sir Robert Scott, the explorer of the pole
For him and his men, there are stories still untold
Of the loneliness and hardships they went through,
To them a hardy word of praise is due.

Remember Alcock and Brown when flying was new
Out over the wild Atlantic those two men flew
With a plane poorly equipped, frail and light
With courage made the first trans-Atlantic flight.

Lindberg was a man of courage, adventure high,
Who fought off sleep so he would not die,
He was in the air both day and night.
Making the first trans-Atlantic solo flight
Many a courageous flyer had tried it before.
They never did make it to the other shore.
It is Lindberg we must give some credit to
He was the first to fly the Atlantic without a crew.

Of squadron leader Bader, Britain should feel proud
For his gallant deed the nation would shout aloud,
A British flyer with two artificial legs he flew,
He crashed his plane but he came back to fly anew
One of England's aces who protected her in the sky
He was the greatest of heroes this no man can deny.

We speak of Robert Bartlett who took Perry to the pole
How he fought the Arctic elements, sleet, wind, rain and cold.
When his ship was stranded, he walked the Chukchi Sea,
To save his men on Wangel Island, Siberia was the key,
He and Kataktovik, an Inuit native, crossed a frozen land
Climbing mountainous icebergs with only rope in hand
Daring perilous ice floes before Siberia came in sight.
Onward they struggled and reached a Chukchi hamlet.
Was here they were greeted with food, cot and blanket.
The word went out, Bartlett crossed the frozen foam.
He stood by his mission, brought his sailors home.

Robert Bartlett's Home Brigus NL

Tunnel Going Through to Bartlett's Cove

Photos by Davis Noel

God Is My Copilot
April 1963

Through the skies of life I must fly alone
And climb high to ascend the unknown,
Up through clouds, against strong winds,
I will stay in the cockpit until life's fuel ends
There is no storm too strong or height too far,
Nor cloud too heavy to black out faith's star,

Through storm clouds low with pockets deep,
With rudder bending, my course I will keep,
I will fly my plane wherever it be,
Over mountain range or tempest sea,
In God, I'll keep faith when tossed about
And I will set as my victor P23* out,

Through clouds of doubt, I shall have no fear
God is my copilot and he is always there.

* Psalm 23

I wrote this poem after watching airplanes at a small airport doing touch and goes, dreaming I was the pilot with only faith in God flying through bad weather. My boyhood dream was to fly a plane.

When The Clock Stops Ticking
January 31, 1963

Tick-tock, tick-tock, tick-tock, tick-tock,
That is the sound of grandfather's clock,
With each ticking moment that's sliding by,
As the new year draws near an old year will die.
Another year of my life is about to begin,
I am another year older, as the clock strikes in,
Out in life's sea I will sail my ship,
With one good canvas, no rail to grip,
They say life's sea is a sea of storm.
I must sail it alone with the coming morn.
From my sister ships I've torn away
I left them at peace in their own little bay.
As I looked behind their lights seemed to motion,
Do not venture alone in that restless ocean.
I am a boy of quest and adventure dare,
My mistakes and failures I want no other to bear,
They say following a storm there is a great calm
Then I hope, to the world, I have proved who I am.
Many ships have been lost on life's restless sea
When the heart of captains wanders aimlessly free,
My ship has one tattered canvas to sail her along
For God is her rudder, mighty and strong.
With hope as bulkhead, faith her mainsail,
Success as homeport, she will not falter or fail,
My ship may look frail, battered and worn
I will sail her safe home with a spirit reborn.
The clock may strike as my years fly by,
I may make a wonder, or even may sigh.
When the clock stops ticking and moments are naught
I hope o'er life's sea, I have my ship safely brought.

I wrote this poem on my 22nd birthday. This was my first birthday in the United States.

Away From Home
January 24, 1963

Tonight I lay away from home
Across the mighty ocean's foam,
I heard a call come from afar
I took it to be my Northern star.

Then by a man-made silver bird
With the impulse in me stirred,
Into God's celestial sky
We headed, that mighty bird and I.

As we pointed to the endless blue
All below looked strange and new
Then I saw before my eyes
As my flight began to rise.

I saw her grandeur and saw it clear,
With running rivers and valleys fair,
The forest below looked devoid of green,
Her hills seemed a shimmering sheen.

Then as we flew toward the coast
I saw below a fervid host,
Stretching both far and wide,
Saw her heart, mind, pulse and pride.

Her sea caps white in her sunset bright
My heart grew heavy as we faded her sight
And as we headed toward the south
I said a prayer as we headed out.

A Light in the Valley
October 22, 1958
For Uncle Augustus Noel

He was a man with life's work done,
His time on earth now spent,
Many times, he read the book of books,
As through his lifetime went,

Now he hears a calling
From his home beyond the sun,
For through his aging body,
Life's blood refused to run.

Lying there on his death bed
With family all gathered round,
All o'er that saddened house,
Was not heard the slightest sound.

He closed his eyes, as if he passed,
And this to him, his son had said,
"Father, you're entering the valley of death."
"Yes, son. I see the Master's light ahead."

He closed his eyes to open no more
For he passed from earth that night,
To enter into that valley of death
To follow God's golden light.

The Robin Red Breast
1962

The robins have returned to this island of ours
They will nest in the treetops and rest in the towers.
You will hear their songs of joy in the air,
Letting us know that spring draws near.
When building their nests of straw and string
We hear them sing by a rippling spring.
Watch as they dig for earthworms deep
While tender care o'er their flock they keep.
When storms roll through on a darkening sky,
On wild spring nights, we see them fly
Warning neighbours from all around
To be prepared for a boisterous sound.

On summer morns as the dawn draws near,
We hear them singing, loud and clear,
With sun shining on red-coated breasts,
We wonder why on this Isle they nest,
For when summer's past, winter is nigh,
Flying southward, some red breasts die.
On cold autumn nights as frost's around
In lone maple tree, an appealing sound,
Tho the flock is gone, one lingers behind,
One little bird a mother can't find.
She stays behind in the wind and cold
To gather her lost child into the fold.

She calls and calls at the top of her voice
She knows the hardships -- knows the price.
With passing days the light grows short
The robin red breast is not of the north.
As nights lengthen, growing cold by the hour,
In the dawn's early morn comes a snow shower.

By now, she's grown so weary and tired
She stood by her family and never retired,
When raising her head to look to the South
A mournful chirp is heard from her mouth.

When opening her wings to fly in the air
As morning lightened, she could only stare.
With one last effort, wings outspread,
She falls to earth, cold, frozen and dead.

I wrote this poem in late autumn after watching a lone robin on a cold and snowy day.

Life's Story Book
March 22, 1958

Life is like a storybook
With pages many and long,
Its chapters full of fun and joy
Others, with unthinkable wrong.
Life may be but a tragedy
Like many books I know,
A message I leave with you,
Pick your title as you go.
As life's storybook comes to an end,
Then the chapters you must close.
For you will have lived the storybook,
The way life comes and goes.

Another day of day dreaming in school.

Give Me A Home In Newfoundland
February 9, 1959

Give me a home in Newfoundland
Where the cod fish live and die,
Salmon go up stream in spring
In autumn the game birds fly.

Give me a home in this caribou land
Where everything's fresh and gay,
You'll find people kind and friendly
As you play in the sun all day.

Give me a home on this little isle
In the mouth of the St. Lawrence tide,
Where the good old Union Jack
Is the Newfoundlanders' pride.

Give me a home in this tenth province
It is not the richest I know,
However, one thing that is sure
People are kind where 'ere you go.

Newfoundland, Newfoundland
You are my island home,
May you forever be
Freedom's beacon in the sea.

God Ne'er Let Us Forget
March 1959

He was but only twenty-four
A young man in his prime,
When the laws of the land upholding
A logger cut short his time.

This young Newfoundlander
Who God looked upon with care,
In the Provincial Police Force
He gave this lad a career.

As he did duty through the night
When walking a city street,
A smile to all he had to give
No matter whom he'd meet.

He was one of twenty transferred,
To the town of Badger, Newfoundland,
Where with the Canadian Mounted Police,
They tried to keep the crowds in hand.

There began the struggle
Between loggers and the law,
The people that night in Badger
This is what they saw.

Suddenly there was a clash
As the men moved to and fro,
And instantly before their eyes
Saw men falling in the snow.

There was one fell that evening
Who would never rise again,
Constable William Moss
That was the victim's name.

For he was a keeper of the law
And God ne'er let us forget,
How this young Newfoundlander
Met a premature death.

This poem is dedicated to Constable William Moss of the Royal Newfoundland Constabulary, killed in Badger, Newfoundland during a logger's union strike.

The Provincial Grand Lodge Session
Held at Freshwater, Newfoundland, February 1906
author unknown

Freshwater will forever be
A green spot in orange history.
The annual meeting held down there
Was represented far and near.

The delegates were men of wit,
Who in that session there did sit,
Not one dull hour there was passed
From the beginning to the last.

Newfoundland may well feel proud
For having such a jolly crowd
Of Orangemen, both North and West,
We claim the smartest and the best.

For instance, there is Capt. Kane,
No smarter king did ever reign
On England's throne, proud may we be
To own such noble men as he.

Such men as Rev. Freeman and Lewis,
All credit then I say is to us
To have such men to fight the wrong,
Victory is certain all along.

Grandmaster Morrison we hold dear
And three times three for him we cheer.
For him who faithfully has been
To all his brother Orangemen.

We cheer again Bro. Piccott,
The man who always holds his wicket,

Bay Roberts Lodge has got a man
That can't be beaten in Newfoundland.

Old Royal Oak, number twenty two,
The mother lodge of all the crew,
Was represented by Langmead
Who for Orange rights did intercede.

Leaming Lodge need fair no crass
While headed by such men as Ash
Victoria chapter, too, I say
Will all feel proud of Sam McBay

Trinity district has n'er before
Had delegates almost a score
And they were lively men tis certain,
Especially Capt. William Martin.

From Dildo Cove to Old Perlican
Every lodge sent forth a man,
But of all the men of Orange race
We missed Elisha Button's face.
.
Letters and telegrams likewise
Came in from some to apologize
For not being able to attend the meeting
And share with us the annual greeting.

Education was well debated,
And past obstacles well related.
Bro. Jordon Milley, all admit
Made such a speech none will forget.

The Rev. Pratt, all will agree,
Is a strong branch on the orange tree.
The Rev. Blount and Codling too,
Are noble Orangemen, firm and true.

No Orangemen will ever flinch
To loudly praise the Rev. Lench
The sermon preached on Jericho wall
Is worthy the praise of one and all.

To all the lodges, North and West,
I simply make but one request
Be steadfast Orangemen, and true
Beneath the yellow, red and blue.

To Grand Bank next we will appear
To help the orange boys up there.
We'll man the ship with Captain Hane
And set the West Coast in a flame.

My few remarks I now must close,
And like Tom Rose I spose I knows
To Freshwater we enjoyed the trip,
And all who went says "Hip: Pip: Pip".

Freshwater: Freshwater: our sad hearts did sigh
As to its kind people we all said goodbye.
But we join hearts and hand and loudly sing
Heaven bless Freshwater and God save the King.

Public domain, author unknown. Captured from an old Toronto paper by Mr. Bill Milley, formerly of Freshwater and now a retired coal miner and living in Glace Bay, N.S., and presented to Walter Simms, a member of the now dormant Lodge Humber of Humbermouth, Newfoundland.

N.B. I found this poem among my father's, Albert Edward Parsons (Ted) Noel's, papers after his death in January 2010.

Orangemen's Parade in Freshwater - early 1900s

Photo found in my grandfather, Charles Butt's photo album.

Life's Mountain
March 18, 1963

Life's mountain is one that is rough and steep,
You must climb it alone every inch of the way,
And life in itself you must struggle to keep,
You must plan in its night to travel its day.

When you look at its top from far down below,
You see not true distance you must ascend,
Where its trails lead you, you will never know,
There are obstructions, hazards at every bend.

As you reach each ledge what will you find?
Disappointment and you again start the climb.
When your joints ache and things slip your mind,
You will realize you are losing your quest with time.

As over life's mountain you scan through a haze
Hope at the last ledge you will not be betrayed
At its top, you will see through sun gleaming rays,
That time lost in your ponder can't 'ere be repaid.

When reaching its crest, you will then take a rest,
You will make your bed for that one final sleep
Tho' ambitious to climb life's mountain crest,
You cannot harvest the seeds you sowed to reap.

For time and illusion derails ambition and plight
As you are ready to reap what you have sown,
You fall asleep in God's slumbering night,
With victory gained, you are too olden grown.
.
When you have conquered life's Matterhorn
Remember the words in God's Book of Books,
"Who ascends the mountain may stand in his holy place,"
Yet man seldom finds peace in all that he looks.

Life's mountain top is so bitter and cold,
When you reach it, you have grown too old.
To do great things you set forth to do,
For time in its might has outwitted you.

What is Life?
1959

What is life but to be born?
To see the sunrise in the morn.
Man is born but a helpless babe
God in it, his own image made.

Life is like a burning ember
Death itself you cannot linger,
The fires of life are kindled low
Choose well the path your soul shall go.

When from out the boundless deep
That call goes out at last to sleep,
To slumber ever in death bound tide
Will you at last with peace abide?

Life must run against time alone
Its hours are to man unknown,
You live today to await tomorrow
Time itself you cannot borrow.

Marching time is an army's might,
Ranks of time no man can smite,
It lays in trenches forward to go,
To reap, destroy, again to sow.

Like the sun in the eastern sky
So is man on earth to die,
As evening shadows fade away
So shall we on Judgment Day.

In the midst of life we are losing out,
With death's dark hour we're still in doubt,
For life is good, but life is strange
Man is lost on its pursuing plains.

You sow today to reap tomorrow,
On life's plain there is grief and sorrow,
You will dream of a harvest bright as gold
Before life's winter on you fold.

What is life if not a dream?
A place for death's lights to gleam.

And lead you out a greater deep
Where life's wages you will reap.

Into this world, we are born
Where our life is first adorn.
As flowers grow and fade away
So shall man in his self same way.

My Beacon Light
April 1979

Often in my dreams at night,
I see a harbour's beacon light,
Guided mariners in darker days
Led them o'er tempestuous waves
A beam that glows in snow and rain,
To set their course for the boundless main,
A flash that raced across the deep
Warning sailors their course to keep.
And as I dream in life's early morn,
I feel a light beam that is warm.
When I awake to a new dawn bright,
I find I too have a beacon light,
That guides me o'er life's harbour strife,
That beacon is my darling wife.

Photo by Justin Noel

Port-de-Grave Lighthouse

I Must Walk This Path Alone
May 17, 1959

I must walk life's path alone
For I am so far from home
I knew not what life would bring
Yet I heard people joyfully sing.

Giving praise to Him above,
Whom the world had given love
Even now as I'm growing old
His story to me is still untold.

I was born of a sinful race
Whom to God we give no grace
O! My soul is full of sin,
Our culture was to cheat to win.

By rules and code of ruthless men
That only taught me crime and sin.
With ebbing life now drifting fast
Found in my heart his joys at last.

His stories at last to me been told
Of gathering sheep into His fold
Now I can sing to Him above
Whom the world gave their love.

I know He will carry me home
Never more to let me roam.
God is good, He will forgive
In His Kingdom let me live.

When I'm gone, turned to dust
Let it be written in God I trust.
We must walk life's path alone
For all our sins, we must atone.

Freshwater United Church

Photo by Justin Noel

Thank You Mom

March 15, 2017

Thank you, Mom, for the love you gave through the years
Blessings you bestowed on me through my hopes and fears

    Into this world, you borne me one cold winter morn
    Swaddling, rocking me keeping me safe and warm.
    And as the years were passing I grew to be a man
    Who had an urge to wander to live in another land.

I remember it was a winter day as winds began to blow
My heart was full of sorrow yet my eyes were all aglow.
I remember you telling me, "Don't let your stay be long.
Live a life that is good and keep away from one of wrong."

Thank you, Mom, for the love you gave through the years
Blessings you bestowed on me through my hopes and fears
But all I could think of through that starry winter night
I was leaving home guided by a mother's shining light.

Thank You Dad
For all Christmases Past
December 2000

Walk me backwards through my dawn's early light
Make me a boy again this Christmas Eve tonight.
Let me lay in my bed in that house on the hill
And wait for the sound of Santa Claus's bell.
I remember the toys you carved out with skill
The horse and the boat that I'd sail in the well.
The trucks and the cars and cap guns that fire
The toys you would fix with wood, glue and wire.
Dad, thank you for all the Christmases past
Their treasures and memories will forever last.

We as a family who live far from your shore
Wish you Merry Christmas and Love Galore.

I wrote this poem in the year after my mother died.

*In Calmness of Evening
Where Autumn Winds Blow
In A Place Called Home*

Freshwater Pond

In The Winds of an Autumn Breeze
1966

I hear you calling, Mother, in winds of an autumn breeze,
Feel the cool Atlantic breezes sweeping over surging seas,
Many a tide has fallen since leaving your rock-bound shore,
Countless dawns have risen, since I heard your billows roar.

As autumn winds are blowing across your mountains high,
I see a lonely seagull soar in a windy cloudy sky,
Hear children singing, as they shared the harvest gain,
Old men telling tales, how they sailed the Spanish Main.

I see creation's wonders through a haloed morning sun
Hear music from your rivers as majestically they run,
A calling of a bull moose ringing through a distant dell
Watched a cunning hunter as he sets forth for the kill.

I have seen your lakes and rivers giving anglers excite,
Seen him journey homeward, in dusk of coming night.
Your nights have many wonders with moons of misty ray,
Dawn shows mystic splendor, as night slips into day.

I hear winds of autumn blowing over barren land,
See scarlet the forest waving at your silver sand,
Hear bell buoys tolling, giving guidance o'er the sea,
I hear you calling mother, calling out to all like me.

Hear you calling, calling, in winds of an autumn breeze,
Calling to your children, to return from life's stormy seas,
When evening tides are rising in a glowing sunset burn,
I will toward your coastline, my weary footsteps turn.

I wrote this poem in Autumn 1966. I was stationed at Lincoln Air Force Base in Lincoln, Nebraska. It was Newfoundland's Come Home Year. Duty called, and I could not get home until late November and by that time the celebrating had ended.

Reflection On The Water
Clowns Cove Pond

Photos by Justin Noel

Photos by Justin Noel

Freshwater School and Community Reunion
August 4th, 2000

On Friday, August 4th, 2000, as the sun was rising over Conception Bay, the citizens of a small scenic community on the rock-bound coast of Newfoundland met dawn's first light with exuberance and fanfare. It was the first day of the Freshwater School and Community Reunion 2000; a day we had all been looking forward to for over a year. It was a day of remembrance for those of us who left our homes many tides ago and now had returned for the momentous event.

Many a sun had risen and many shadows of evening had faded since some of us had last seen each other and now we were given this opportunity to see, talk, and walk with one another once again. It was a time as the poet once said to, "Backward, turn backward, O Time, in your flight and make me a boy again just for tonight." Turn backward is just what we did, back to the days of our childhood, back to the memories of a time past when we played Hopscotch, Kick the Stone, Wheel the Hoop, Whip the Top, swam, rode our bikes, played ball and went to school. It was here on winter evenings we went nansarying and sleding, skating, played hockey, and walked the streets with our girl and boyfriends, when the only sounds to be heard were the tolling of the bell buoy near Carbonear Island, warning the mariners of treacherous shoals, and the scrunching of the frozen snow beneath our feet. We all remembered the Christmases of our youth when we went partying, dancing and janneying. These were the memories we all relived in a space of a three-day period in this small picturesque historic community.

The celebrations began with registration at the church school hall where we were entertained by local community bands throughout the day. At the Orange Lodge a museum was set up. A display was arranged of old pictures of Freshwater, Flatrock, Blow Me Down and Otterbury and many interesting relics of a gone by era. The local craftsmen proudly presented their model boats and houses and others told their stories of what life was like growing up in this community seventy or eighty years ago. It was a time to listen and a time to remember, for it will soon be our time to pass those stories on to our children and to our children's children, for there can be no future without a past and there can be no past without a future.

As that first day faded into evening, we were served hot delicious homemade soup followed by the opening ceremonies where we were presented a colour guard made up of the Canadian, United States and Newfoundland flags. Local singers sang the national anthems: O Canada, Star Spangler Banner and the Ode to Newfoundland. Two citations were presented to the town from the Commonwealth of Massachusetts: one from the Governor, which reads in part, *TO THE TOWN OF FRESHWATER CARBONEAR NEWFOUNDLAND - In recognition of your history and altruistic contributions to the Commonwealth of Massachusetts.*; and a second from the House of Representatives together with a state flag which reads in part, *TO THE TOWN OF FRESHWATER CARBONEAR NEWFOUNDLAND - In recognition of the strength and heart of the community in this outstanding town, and its extended and enduring relationship with the Commonwealth of Massachusetts.* This is the first time in recorded Newfoundland history that a Citation was received from the Commonwealth of Massachusetts and presented to the citizens of a town in the Province of Newfoundland and Labrador. Local community bands, concerts and comedies followed late into the night.

Saturday morning, as the sun shone brightly on this quaint seacoast community, many of us were back in the church hall being served a Fish and Brewis breakfast. Mmm, Mmm, was it ever good. The rest of the day was much like Friday. We listened to local community bands and a variety of entertainment and much time was spent conversing with old and new friends. Early Saturday evening we were served a hot roast beef dinner and later in the evening, on Clowns Cove Beach where an estimated fifteen hundred people had gathered, we were presented with a night to remember. It was Dance Time. We danced all night as the bands played on into the wee hours of the morning. It was a night when the Forties, Fifties, Sixties, and Seventies, all the way to the millennium came alive in the cool night air. If you were standing, you were dancing. The beach was electrified with the sound of music as it ricocheted off the surrounding hills and echoed across the waters. The jannies were there, the local community bands, singers and comedians and jokers were there along with the Mr. and Mrs. Freshwater Pageant. The young and the old, the locals and the visitors alike enjoyed sound and sights that night on Clowns Cove Beach. Just hours before the dawn we departed to our places of rest.

Saturday's cool dark night faded into the warmth of a Sunday morning sunrise. We rose early finding ourselves once again in the church hall, this time being served a hot breakfast of bacon, eggs, tea, coffee and toast. After breakfast the church bell rang out its call to the people to come and worship. It was like a time past as three hundred or more filled the church pews and when the congregation rose to sing, one could only think back to the time when our forefathers sang their praises. It was like an answer to the echo from their songs of long ago and one could only be moved when the choir sang, "My eyes have seen the glory of the coming of the Lord. He is trampling out the vintage where the grapes of wrath are stored." I can still hear the low flowing music and the soft synchronized voices of the choir and the muffled thump, thump foot beat of the congregation, as they sang with feeling far beyond description. In the afternoon we gathered at the Freshwater Cemetery on McCanister's Hills, one of Newfoundland's best-manicured cemeteries, where we paid our respects to those who had gone before. The members of the Royal Canadian Legion were in attendance and performed a remembrance ceremonial. Wreaths were laid in memory of the Freshwater servicemen who paid the supreme sacrifice in time of war. When the bugler played "The Last Post" we stood in silence for a moment of reverence and reflection. As its lingering notes echoed in the hills we parted ways once again. We said our goodbyes and we all agreed a good time was had by all. Some time down life's road may we all meet again?

We know that fifty years from now, Saturday, August 6, 2050, there will be another gathering at the Freshwater Cemetery on McCanister's Hills; it will be for recovery of the time capsule that was placed there during the School and Community Reunion 2000.

To those who will be in attendance fifty years from now I ask you to never forget the past. In that capsule are many items of historical and personal reflection. This information has been placed there so you may pass it on to your children and your children's children. For all of us who have walked these hills and down these valleys, strolled along these beaches in the cool night air and watched the sunrise as a new day dawns, we can feel the bonds of our birth to A Place Called Home – Freshwater, Conception Bay North.

wwww.Freshwater-Carbonear.com

Come Home Year 2000

Opening Ceremonies - Jannies on Clowns Cove Beach
Placing of time capsule to be opened in 2050

William Noel's House
Built 1881

Root Celler Built about 1800

Strolling Arm in Arm
In A Place Called Home

Pictures from the Old Family Album

Aunt Jane and Uncle Willis Noel

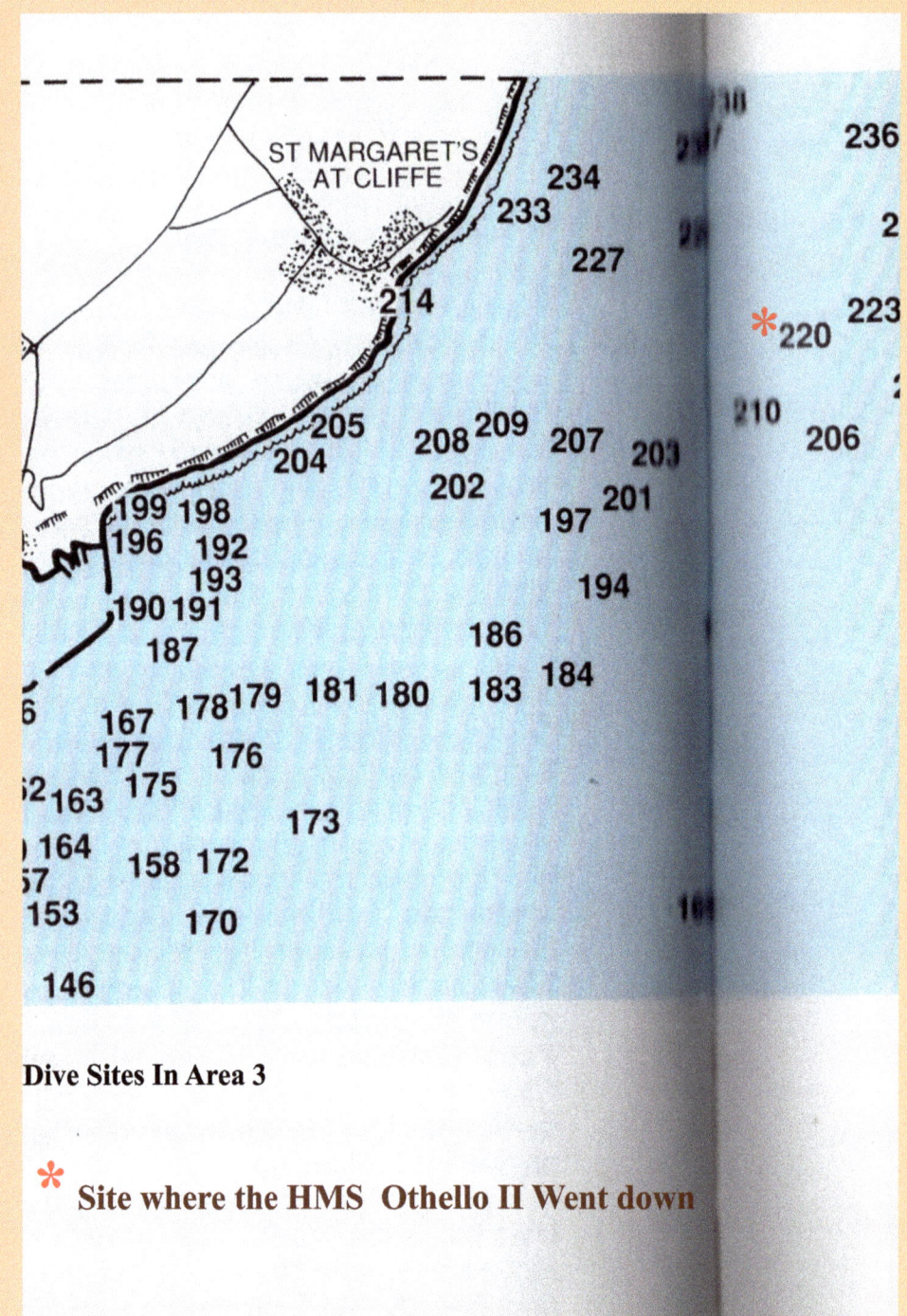

Dive Sites In Area 3

* Site where the HMS Othello II Went down

The Fate of the Emden
German Battleship

The picture on page 17 shows the engagement of the German Battleship "Emden" by the Australian Cruiser which was built by the people of Australia. The "Emden" had a remarkable career for a short time and inflicted considerable loss on British commerce. It was one of the fastest ships in the German Navy and consequently managed for some time to keep clear of any British vessels with which it did not desire to try conclusion contenting itself with preying upon the helpless merchantmen of the British Marine. Fortunately, the Australian Cruiser succeeded in cornering the "Emden" with the result that it was driven ashore and destroyed and the crew captured.

This picture gives a very realistic view of the sea fight which is one that will long be remembered, to the honour and glory of the British Navy and to the credit of the Australian Cruiser.

A View From The Old Cemetery

Goats on Freshwater Hill

1982

Library, Archives, Museum and other Sources.

Picture Index

Great Britain UK

Page 14	Courtesy of DIVER Group Magazine – Eaton Publication
Page 6,39,42,43	Permission of Imperial War Museum (IWM)
Page 45	Courtesy of Royal Air Force Museum
Page 8,12,26,33 34,38	Courtesy of Commonwealth War Graves Commission

United States

Page 62	Courtesy of National Archives and Records Administration
Page 71	Courtesy of US Navy National Museum of Naval Aviation
Page 52	Courtesy of US Naval History & Heritage Command
Page 61	Courtesy of National Museum of the U.S. Air Force
Page 65	Wikimedia Commons, free media repository Photo in *Public Domain*

Canada

Page 11,46	Courtesy of Library and Archives Canada
Page 68	Permission of Canadian War Museum
Page 18	Courtesy of Veterans Affairs Canada
Page 5	Courtesy of National Film Board of Canada/Library and Archives

Newfoundland

Page IX,23	Courtesy of Frank Gogos/The Veteran Magazine
Page 43	Courtesy of Grand Banks Genealogy Site
Page 44	Courtesy of Grand Falls-Windsor Heritage Society
Page 47	Courtesy of Thornhill Photography
Page 150	Digitized Maps from the Centre for Newfoundland Studies Memorial University of Newfoundland

Other Sources

Memorial University of Newfoundland (MUN)
The Royal Newfoundland Regiment Museum
Newfoundland Quarterly
The Twillingate Sun

Roland Noël was born in Freshwater, Conception Bay, Newfoundland on January 31, 1941. His formative years - during World War II and pre-confederation with Canada - were a time of momentous change: the merging of past and present, modern and vintage. It was from this place, Roland began to write poems to appreciate and understand the rugged, creative, and spirited people of Newfoundland. At age 22, he left Freshwater and moved to the United States, serving with the United States Air Force during the Vietnam War. After an honorable discharge, he had a successful career in Information Technology. Today, he resides in Tewksbury, Massachusetts with his wife, Eve. They make a yearly pilgrimage to their ancestral home each summer.

Christian Noel

www.ingramcontent.com/pod-product-compliance
Lightning Source LLC
Chambersburg PA
CBHW041310240426
43661CB00064B/2887